Beyond the Centaur

Auguste Rodin's sculpture *The Thinker*, created for *The Gates of Hell*, a visual depiction of a scene from Dante's *Inferno*. *The Thinker*, a 27″ painted plaster figure seated above the scene, represented Dante contemplating the figures below. The sculpture was originally named by Rodin *The Poet*. The first over-life-sized bronze enlargement of the figure was done in 1904. A casting of *The Thinker* was placed on Rodin's tomb in Meudon, where it served as headstone and epitaph.

Beyond the Centaur

Imagining the Intelligent Body

MARGARET R. MILES

CASCADE *Books* • Eugene, Oregon

BEYOND THE CENTAUR
Imagining the Intelligent Body

Cascade Books
An Imprint of Wipf and Stock Publishers
199 W. 8th Ave., Suite 3
Eugene, OR 97401

www.wipfandstock.com

ISBN 13: 978-1-62564-420-6

Cataloging-in-Publication data:

Miles, Margaret R. (Margaret Ruth), 1937–

Beyond the centaur : imagining the intelligent body / Margaret
R. Miles.

xvi + 132 p. ; 23 cm. —Includes bibliographical references and
indexes.

ISBN 13: 978-1-62564-420-6

1. Human body (Philosophy)—History. 2. Descartes, René,
1596–1650—Influence. I. Title.

BL51 .M54 2014

Manufactured in the U.S.A.

For Owen Thomas

Contents

Preface

Serious and extended study of a subject may well turn up findings that are radically incompatible with popular beliefs and attitudes.

—MAXINE SHEETS-JOHNSTONE[1]

The centaur is a mythological figure, usually a man, with a human head and torso, joined at the waist to the body of a horse. The centaur was described in ancient literature and sculpture as perpetually struggling with its two natures; wild as an untamed horse, he was also a civilized human. Barbarism and wisdom were constantly in violent conflict for ascendency. Although the centaur was usually depicted as powerful and fiercely aggressive, in some myths he was described as a wise teacher. The appeal of the myth of the centaur and its longevity in art and literature reveal humans' alleged internal struggle between the "lower appetites" and civilization, a struggle represented as incompatible body parts. Human beings, the myth states, are centaurs.

The myth of the centaur pictures a pervasive flaw carrying major consequences that runs like a fault line

1. Sheets-Johnstone, *Corporeal Turn*, 49.

through Western philosophy and theology. Too large to be visible to the naked eye, hidden in full view, the assumption is that persons are composed of components of unequal value—body and soul or rational mind. This assumption informs our experience of moving, feeling, believing, thinking, and even dying. Values associated with our alleged different "components" follow inevitably and apparently irresistibly. Other suggestions about what a person *is* have not been successful in unseating the dominant assumption that we are centaurs.

Although historians usually focus on *differences* between societies, continuities are even more significant than differences and more challenging to understand and explain. One of the continuities that struck me as I studied and taught history for many years was the virtually unquestioned assumption—up to our own time—that we humans are hastily assembled *parts*. No one defined with any precision what those parts are, or what relation they bear to one another, but from the pre-Socratics to the postmodernists, *they kept trying*. Why has it seemed evident to generations that persons are parts? Having puzzled over it obsessively for years, I think that part of the incentive for this assumption is experiential, emerging from a persistent experience of discomfort and disorientation in the world. "Human beings are deeply troubled about being human," Martha Nussbaum writes, "about being highly intelligent and resourceful, on the one hand, but weak and vulnerable, helpless against death, on the other."[2] To explain this experience of awkwardness and discomfort to ourselves we imagine that our *parts* are

2. Nussbaum, *Hiding from Humanity*, 336.

inharmonious, if not actively in conflict, that we are, as it has often been put, both angels and beasts, centaurs. Or our experience may be explained as the result of our existence in a profoundly alien world: "This world is not my home, I'm just a-passing through," as the song puts it. In either case we struggle for legitimacy and authenticity, for orientation, for comfort, for a feeling of belonging. As the French phrase articulates it, we struggle for "*bien dans ma peau*" (well-being in my skin).

One result of the mistake of conceptualizing persons as components is the separation of thinking and life experience in academic work. We scholars strive for "objectivity." I suspect that many or most of us long to bring the subjects we study into closer conversation with our life experience. We long to think with our intelligent bodies, with our whole experience. Alas, we have not been taught responsible methods for doing so, and we have few models. We have been taught to be scrupulous about acknowledging the sources of the *ideas* that inform our thinking, but we have no method for identifying and acknowledging the *experiences* that prompt and direct our interests. Perhaps we have simply not recognized the value of exploring the connection of what and how we think to the color and texture of our lives, the "silken weavings of our afternoons,"[3] the many people and experiences that shape us and direct our attention. To think with the intelligent body, rather than the rational mind isolated from our experience and feelings, is to think more honestly and transparently. Is it possible to feel our thoughts and

3. Stevens, "Sunday Morning," in *Collected Poems*, 66.

think our feelings?[4] Chapters 5 and 6 imagine an activity in which thinking and feeling are no longer separated.[5]

Far from being a new idea, even though shunned in twenty-first-century academic circles, the mutually informing activities of thought and life were recognized long ago. Epictetus (ca. 55–135 CE), a Greek slave, who has been called "the most acute mind . . . among the late Stoics," considered thinking an art (*technè*), "a particular kind of craftsmanship, perhaps to be deemed the highest—certainly the most urgently needed, because its end product is the conduct of your own life."[6]

The myth of the centaur prompted me to consider its alternative. I asked myself, if we conceptualized ourselves as intelligent bodies instead of as centaurs, how would we *move* differently? How would we *feel* differently? How would we *think* differently? Would we feel our thoughts and think our feelings? How would we *believe* differently? What if belief is not assent of the rational mind, as we usually assume, but a practice of the intelligent body, the *person*, undivided and indivisible? In each chapter I conduct what Hannah Arendt has called a "thought experiment"; I try to imagine how we would *live and die differently* if we

4. The philosophers Paul and Patricia Churchland "like to try . . . to believe that they themselves are thoroughly physical creatures but also to *feel it*—to experience their thoughts as bodily sensations" (MacFarquhar, "Two Heads").

5. Kirsch refers to T. S. Eliot's complaint that "modern poets had lost the ability to feel their thoughts and think their feelings" ("On Bellow's *Henderson the Rain King*, 54).

6. Arendt, *Thinking*, 154. Pierre Hadot's *Philosophy as a Way of Life* also describes Plotinus's philosophy as specifically directed to living well.

thought of ourselves as intelligent bodies rather than as rational minds uneasily glued to recalcitrant bodies.

The fourth-century theologian Augustine of Hippo appears frequently in these pages. Augustine is a historical author whose writings have alternatively dazzled and annoyed me for many years. Although he insisted that soul and body are distinct and that soul is "better than" body, his writings nevertheless reveal his "silent thought" of their mutual interdependence. It is often amusing to see his translators struggle for clarity that cannot be traced to his native Latin, for precision that reflects the translator's loyalties more than it does his statements. To translate is inevitably to interpret. I am no exception, so I should confess my bias: I translate and/or interpret Augustine at the vivid end of the continuum of meaning of his language. Whether sinner or saint, he was a passionate man, full of life. "*Inardescimus et imus*," he said: "We are inflamed and we go!"[7]

As I contemplated and endeavored to organize this book, I experienced a disjunction between rational thought and physical feeling in a particularly intense way. My husband, ninety years old, was suffering from dementia, exacerbated by hearing and memory loss. As his dementia increased, so did my exhaustion. I asked his twin sons (age fifty-seven) and my daughter (age fifty-six) for a family consultation. All agreed that the time was right for him to enter an assisted living residence. I determined to keep my attention on the relief I would experience when

---

7. A description of my long engagement with Augustine's writings can be found in my book *Augustine and the Fundamentalist's Daughter*.

I would no longer be his primary caregiver. But emotionally this was not the whole story.

I was alone when the full weight of *sadness* came over me. I realized that I probably would not, in future, live with someone with whom I had lived for thirty-one years. I fainted or, as my physician put it, I experienced a "vasovagal event." In the seconds of dizziness preceding my fall, I clutched at things in order to remain standing—exactly the wrong thing to do—thus complicating the fall, so that it produced several broken and cracked ribs, a sprained hand, and a colorful, so-called black eye. My rational mind quickly explained the episode as the result of an encounter between two incompatible feelings, relief and sadness. Rational mind can quickly name and explain almost any event. "Thought is swift, clearly, because it is immaterial, and this in turn goes a long way toward explaining the hostility of the great metaphysicians to their own bodies. From the viewpoint of the thinking ego, the body is nothing but an obstacle."[8]

Body heals at a slower pace. "Ribs take three months," my doctor said. The difference in the pace of mind and body contributes to our sense that we are *composed* of two separate entities. We who exercise and treasure rational mind are surprised and affronted when we are forced to submit to body's snail's pace. Can we discipline rational mind to *think with* the emotions it excludes in order to think rapidly? Why would we want to? Simply to overcome the awkward and painful sense of being "components," in order to experience the wholeness of the intelligent body.

8. Arendt, *Thinking*, 44.

Acknowledgments

Since my retirement, conversation partners and critical friends have become more important than ever. No longer are classrooms full of intelligent and creative students on hand to ponder and discuss my ideas. Learned colleagues no longer converse over lunch several days each week. Thus, I needed and appreciated friends who listened and responded to my repetitive rants about the "intelligent body," especially Judith Berling, Susan Burris, Leslie Ewing, Siduri Haslerig, Flora Keshgegian, William Rankin, Martha Stortz, and Susan Suntree. I gave lectures based on early stages of *Beyond the Centaur* at the (Episcopal) Northern California Clergy Conference in May 2013, receiving valuable feedback there. And Mary Hunt invited me to speak at a WATER teleconference in which my ideas were exposed for comments that were helpful and encouraging and that gave me energy to continue writing at a time when life circumstances were difficult. To each person who listened and talked back, my great gratitude.

PART ONE

From Stacked Components to the Intelligent Body

1

Introduction

Philosophy and theology are only as good as the an-thropology they assume. The idea of "person" we have inherited in the West assumes that persons consist of two (or more) assembled, stuck together, hierarchically arranged components, usually body and mind or soul. Other components, such as spirit, may be added; we're not very clear about these parts and their roles. A "silent thought,"[1] namely, that persons consist of two entities, directs our physical movements, our feelings, our thoughts, how we believe, and how we approach death.

If instead we conceptualized ourselves as intelligent bodies—*indivisible, not analyzable into parts, one entity*—how might we experience our lives differently? In this book I will undertake the difficult (because seldom practiced and lacking models) exercise of thinking as an intelligent body rather than as a rational mind. To think with the intelligent body is to reunite rational thought, traditionally assigned to mind, and emotion, traditionally

1. Michel Foucault's phrase for an unexamined assumption.

assigned to body. *Beyond the Centaur* is not an argument but an exploration, an exercise.[2] Its goal is to provoke other thought experiments in imagining intelligent bodies.

I

For many centuries it has seemed self-evident to philosophers and theologians that persons are made up of components; until recently it has also seemed indisputable to most that mind or soul must rule the ensemble, "mastering" the recalcitrant body. In Part One, I sketch with a broad brush the gradual development of the idea of persons as components from the pre-Socratics to Descartes, the first author in which the *distinction* explicitly became a *separation*.

Presently, however, not everyone stacks our assumed components in the same way. Toward the end of the twentieth century, a number of theologians championed the "absent body," endeavoring to rescue body from its bad press in historical Christianity.[3] And contemporary neurophysiologists and some philosophers consider mind an epiphenomenon of body, dependent on body for its physical operations as well as its perspective. Turning the traditional idea of person upside down, they place body in the commanding position; soul receives orders from body. While Plato said, "The body is the prison-

---

2. Arendt, *Willing*, 166.

3. The title of Drew Leder's book *The Absent Body*. A short list includes Joel Green, Melanie May, M. Shawn Copeland, and the contributors to Althaus-Reid and Isherwood's edited volume *Controversies in Body Theology*.

house of the soul,"[4] Antonio Damasio writes, "the brain is the *body's* captive audience."[5] "Biological drives, body states, and emotions [are] an indispensable foundation for rationality," he writes.[6] Not only is rationality the "helpless victim" of body; feelings and emotions also depend on body, and "emotion is integral to the process of reasoning and decision-making."[7] However, theologians, neurophysiologists, and philosophers all seem to take for granted that persons are two things, at least two things.

Given this remarkable consensus across centuries, I was intrigued and fascinated to find a philosopher who argues that we are irreducibly *one* thing—an *intelligent body* that cannot be dissected or analyzed into parts. Maxine Sheets-Johnstone—contemporary philosopher, dancer, evolutionary biologist, phenomenologist, and developmental psychologist—understands human persons as being on a continuum of human and nonhuman animals, intelligent bodies all. Moreover, thinking of persons as intelligent bodies challenges the gender assumptions that have organized Western societies, in which men are associated with rational thought and women with body and emotion. If the dissection of persons into mind/soul and body doesn't work, neither do traditional gender arrangements nor the socialization that renders gendered social arrangements "natural." In Part II, I explore suggestions and practices that presume another model, namely, that we are "one thing," an intelligent body.

4. Plato, *Cratylus* 400c; *Gorgias* 493a.

5. Damasio, *Descartes' Error*, xv.

6. Ibid., 200

7. Damasio, *Feeling of What Happens*, 41.

Rational thought, the activity of the allegedly detachable soul/mind, is a difficult and laborious *learned* activity, a skill developed under historical conditions that cannot be discussed fully here. Picture Rodin's sculpture *The Thinker*: The thinker's body is tense and cramped, struggling to produce rational thought. From this immense physical effort, humans developed—gradually, over centuries—the ability to isolate rationality and to plot its operation: logic. No longer was thinking the result of *physical* effort; we humans learned to think with our rational minds, with our minds *only*, assigning emotion to body and excluding body and emotion from the activity of thinking. We call this "objectivity" and we are very proud of its accomplishment. It took centuries, but we did it! Now we find it "natural." As the song says, "It's second nature to me now, like breathing out and breathing in . . ." Nevertheless, it is not natural but learned behavior.

When I retired from a teaching career I trained as a hospice volunteer. Having examined conceptions of bodies for many years, I wanted to be with actual bodies—not presently the warm, milky-smelling bodies of my little children, but the bodies of persons in their last months, weeks, or days of life. I wanted to hear life stories, to warm cold hands, and to rub lotion into dry feet. The criterion for a patient qualifying for hospice care was her doctor's best guess that she would live no longer than six months. Yet I found that patients could not be considered "dying people." They were, rather, living people who wanted to live each day as fully and richly as possible. My task was to find the activities that would enable that particular richness for *that* patient on *that* day. Hospice volunteering taught me something both intimate and concrete about intelligent living/dying bodies like my own. Neither mind in isolation nor body in isolation is a trustworthy and fruitful source of understanding and living; the reality of human persons is intelligent bodies.

II

Why did historical authors speak so consistently of body and soul as opposing entities? The answer, no doubt, is endlessly complex, and I will consider answers to this question as they arise. The answer has partly to do with resentment of body in a time in which "pain management" was virtually nonexistent, surgery was performed without anesthetic, and lacking antibiotics, people died of what we today would consider small infections.

Uncontrollable vulnerability and unrelieved suffering might have been reason enough for historical people to resent the diseased or damaged body. But it was not only the body in pain that they resented; they also grew tired of the constant and laborious maintenance required by healthy bodies: the necessity of finding food and lacking refrigeration, consuming it before it spoiled; for women, hazardous childbearing; for men, as well as women and children, the threat and reality of war. In these hazardous circumstances, people were not inclined to focus on "spirituality"—*thus* the frequent admonishments in the Christian West to overlook, to look over or "transcend," body.

Moreover, we who live in a belligerently hedonistic public culture may find it difficult to recognize that for many (perhaps most) historical people most of the time, sex was a mixed blessing. Lacking effective methods of birth control, many women suffered from frequent and debilitating pregnancy and childbearing. And by the sixteenth century, an epidemic of syphilis made sex dangerous and potentially lethal for everyone.

Language is a rough tool with which to try to understand historical people and their ideas. We cannot assume that a word (in translation) means today what it meant when it was written. For example, historical people understood *opposite* and *opposing* differently than we do. Attention to context often reveals that the writer used these words to describe entities that depend on one another and work together—like body and soul. We still use the word in that way when we speak of the *opposable* thumb in relation to the fingers. For the intelligent body, however, there are no "parts" that work together and depend on each other; there is no "they."

But something more intimate and immediate lies beneath efforts to distance our-*selves* from our bodies, namely, the fear of death. Bodies are exposed, vulnerable to pain, disease, and suffering, out of one's control.[8] According to the "components" model of person, death involves a violent and painful tearing apart of soul/mind and body.[9] In chapter 8 I consider how death might be imagined and approached differently by the intelligent body.

---

8. Sheets-Johnstone, *Roots of Morality*, 52.

9. Augustine called death a "harsh and acerbic" experience (*City of God*, 13.6).

III

Is it merely an academic exercise to question centuries of assumptions about the human person? The separation of persons into components of unequal value has had and is having effects on American society that are too fundamental and too large to document. Can the effects of that "silent thought" be identified?

In *The Social Health of the Nation: How America Is Really Doing*,[10] Marc and Marque-Luisa Miringoff argue that although Americans receive constant reports on the nation's economic health, reports on the nation's social health are few and episodic. Social health, they write, can be measured by assessing sixteen factors, such as "the well-being of America's children and youth, the accessibility of health care, the quality of education, the adequacy of housing, the security and satisfaction of work, and the nation's sense of community, citizenship, and diversity." The Miringoffs say that if such social data were regularly reported, Americans would have to acknowledge that several key social factors have worsened significantly over time and are currently performing at levels far below what was achieved in previous decades. According to the sixteen social indicators, social conditions were best in the early 1970s, worsened during the early 1980s, and improved in the late 1990s. Bringing their analysis up to 2010, the last year for which data was analyzed, they report no progress in the last decade. American society is becoming meaner by the day to the young, the old, the vulnerable, and the marginal.

10. Published by The Institute for Innovation in Social Policy, originally at Fordham University, presently housed at Vassar College.

- Suicide rates among the young are 36 percent higher than they were in 1970.

- Income inequality is at its third worst level in fifty years.

- More than 41 million Americans are without health insurance, the worst performance since records have been kept.

- Violent crime remains almost double what it was in 1970.

- Average wages for American workers have fallen sharply since the early 1970s.

- Child abuse has increased dramatically.

- Approximately one in every five children in America today lives in poverty, a 33 percent increase since 1970. America has the highest child poverty rate in the industrialized world.

- Twenty-nine industrialized nations have lower infant mortality than the United States.

- By the beginning of the twenty-first century America's gross domestic product had risen 140 percent over its 1970 amount, but in the same period America's social health decreased by 38 percent.[11]

In sum, it is urgent *in American society, at this time*, to value and care for vulnerable persons. Sheets-Johnstone has suggested that we lose the concept of person when we imagine persons as compiled components. The present condition of the social health of America strongly indicates that we have indeed lost the concept of persons, intelligent bodies, for whom food, health care, and education are highly and equally important.

11. Miringoff and Miringoff, *Social Health of the Nation*, 5.

IV

The problem of religious belief runs like a *leitmotif* through the chapters that follow. Although (many) Americans (sometimes) take "on faith" the claims made by advertisers and scientists, religious beliefs are suspect in secular public society. We think that religion is all about consent to creedal statements. We assume that something called mind must assent to religious claims, and our (pseudo) scientific intellectual culture rejects claims that are unsupported by evidence. So we deny ourselves the orientation, comfort, and challenge offered by religious beliefs. Religious belief is seldom considered *primarily* a way of life, an intelligent body's choice of lifestyle in twenty-first-century America.

An example: The Christian claim that bodies will be resurrected after death is central to Christian faith but is *believed* by almost no one. In fact, in approximately two thousand years of the Christian movement, *no* progress has been made in understanding and explaining this doctrine. By contrast, the doctrine of original sin is amply documented. G. K. Chesterton once remarked that original sin is the only Christian doctrine that is well documented; any newspaper, on any day, will provide abundant evidence. There is no evidence whatsoever of the resurrection of body. It is a matter of *belief*, not knowledge. The best the rational mind can do with the claim that bodies will be resurrected after death is to *practice the discipline of agnosticism*. However, as discussed in chapters 7 through 9, intelligent bodies *can* believe in this doctrine.

V

What could be regarded as imprecise use of language (from the perspective of the components model) unwittingly reveals that intelligent body's activities are sometimes almost indistinguishable. We say we "know" when we mean "believe" (as in "I know that my redeemer lives"). We say "believe" when we mean "think" ("I believe I'll go shopping now"). We say "think" when we are "feeling" and "feel" when we are "thinking." Is this simply sloppy, or is there a deeper wisdom in popular usage? Because the intelligent body model does not assign these activities to a designated part of the person (thinking and believing to rational mind, and feeling and movement to body), it is less tempting to distinguish them. Nonetheless, *description* requires potentially falsifying analysis. We usually conflate description with reality; I will try to demonstrate the imprecision of distinctions as I discuss the holistic activities of the intelligent body.

Books are addressed to rational minds. Therefore the contents of a book should be organized according to the logical progression of the book's argument. However, this book's organization is incongruent with its argument. The table of contents implies that movement, thinking, feeling, and believing can be discussed serially. It surreptitiously smuggles in the very concept of person that it pretends to jettison, implying that these activities are distinguishable, if not separable, activities belonging to different "parts" of the person. The book's thesis, however, is that this is not the case.

Like Plato's "dividing line," the moving, thinking, feeling, and believing intelligent body can be divided only conceptually. In "reality," these activities are not "they" at all, but the unified activity of the intelligent body. Does an infant "decide" that it is time to roll over or start walking? Does she "believe" that the floor will remain stable to accept her footsteps? Does she articulate, even to herself, the "I can" feeling? Until each of us is taught to compartmentalize, we move, feel, think, and believe simultaneously and with great confidence.

Do we conceptualize persons as components because of our experience of disunity and discomfort? Or do we experience disunity and discomfort because we conceptualize persons as parts? If the latter, could a change in the way we conceptualize ourselves enable and encourage nondualistic *experience*, the experience of intelligent bodies that simultaneously think and feel, move and believe? I explore that possibility in the following chapters.

2

Before Descartes

When Socrates goes home he is not alone,
he is by himself.
—HANNAH ARENDT[1]

A brief and necessarily simplified retracing of the steps by which persons came to be thought of as components is preliminary to exploration of how our lives might be different if we thought of ourselves as intelligent bodies. Western philosophy and Christianity have consistently assumed an "indestructible and immortal" soul and a biodegradable body.[2] We have assigned value and reality to soul and urged that body be, at best, ignored, at worst, actively disparaged, if not harmed. A lengthy and inevitably boring demonstration of the consistency

---

1. Arendt, *Thinking*, 187.

2. For a learned discussion of theological claims about the composition of persons from the Bible to the present, see Green, *Body, Soul, and Human Life*.

of this "silent thought"[3] underlying Western conceptions of "person" need not be done here. A couple of examples will suffice. "When body flourishes, soul withers," said one fourth-century desert ascetic.[4] A thousand years later Thomas à Kempis wrote, "The more the body is reduced by suffering, the more the spirit is strengthened." He added, "It is a wretched thing to live on earth. . . . [T]he needs of the body in this world are certainly a great burden to the soul."[5]

Pre-Socratics

Pre-Socratic philosophers apparently effortlessly blended religious and scientific inquiry, assuming no division between matter and spirit, but a mutual and essential interdependence.[6] Aeschylus wrote,

> The pure sky [Ouranos] desires to penetrate the earth, and the earth is filled with love so that she longs for blissful union with the sky. The rain falling from the beautiful sky impregnates the earth, so that she gives birth to plants and grain for beasts and men.[7]

In the extant fragments of pre-Socratic philosophers' writings, the language of body and soul/mind is not absent, but their *agenda* insists on the mutual attraction and interdependency of body and soul. Like the "opposable"

3. Foucault's term. See *Use of Pleasure*, 9.
4. *Sayings of the Fathers*, in Chadwick, *Western Ascetism*, 109.
5. Thomas à Kempis, *Imitation*, 70.
6. Wheelwright, *Presocratics*, 1.
7. Ibid., 17.

thumb, working in concert with the fingers, the "opposition" of spiritual and material, sky and earth, is a working arrangement. In reality, Thales said, "All things are full of gods,"[8] and "the earth is one."[9] They sought a common material basis of all things: Thales proposed water, Heraclitus proposed fire, and Anaximenes proposed air.

Even while insisting on the essential unity of all things, the pre-Socratic philosophers found that the *articulation* of this unity must involve the interplay of opposites, like two sides of a coin, or two faces of a column statue. However, *description is not reality*. To close the gap between description and reality a further step is needed, namely, recognition that the moving parts are, in reality, one entity. Heraclitus's best effort to describe the unity of all things involved asserting that there must be *two parts*, but that there is, in reality, only *one thing*: "All things come to be by conflict between opposites, and the universe in its entirety flows like a river." Soul, he said, is "the vaporization out of which everything else is composed . . . it is the least corporeal of things and is in constant flux [like everything else]."[10] In short, it is not that the universe itself is *composed* of *components,* but *description* of its unity requires its analysis into parts.

8. Ibid., 45.
9. Ibid., 51.
10. Heraclitus, Frag. 12, in ibid., 82

Platonists

Plato's *Phaedo* is the classic text in which Socrates argues
for the immortality of soul, and thus its consummate value. In a dialogue with Cebes, Socrates' argument unfolds:

> Tell me, what must be present in a body to make
> it alive?
> Soul.
> Is this always so?
> Of course.
> So whenever soul takes possession of a body, it
> always brings life with it?
> Yes, it does.
> Is there an opposite to life, or not?
> Yes, there is.
> What?
> Death.
> Does it follow , then, . . . that soul will never ad-
> mit the opposite of that which accompanies it?
> Most definitely . . .
> And what do we call that which does not admit
> death?
> Immortal.
> And soul does not admit death?
> No.
> So soul is immortal.
> Yes, it is immortal. . . .
> Can we say that that has been proved? What do
> you think?
> Most completely, Socrates.[11]

Minutes before his own death Socrates is reported
to have said, "The mortal part of us dies, but the im-

---

11. Plato, *Phaedo,* 105d-e, in *Collected Dialogues.*

mortal part retires at the approach of death and escapes unharmed and indestructible."[12]

Plato shared the pre-Socratics' penchant for describing *a unity* by analyzing it into *parts*. He reminded his readers that the "divided line" between "the intelligible order" and "the world of the eyeball" arbitrarily designates, not different realities, but different *methods* of approach. Study of the intelligible order requires the method of dialectic, or reasoning based on information garnered from the visible world. Study of the visible world consists of vision, observation, and description. The so-called divided line is purely conceptual, a clumsy *representation* of reality, not reality itself.[13]

I speculate that the primary reason many scholars seek to trace the ideas they study back to Plato is that his writings are the first explicitly to treat body (within "the world of the eyeball") and soul (belonging to the intelligible order) as *distinguishable* entities. Even while we criticize his "dualism," scholars recognize that Plato shares the worldview that underlies our own. Ignoring his careful attempt to acknowledge that description is not reality, we cast out, as the Scripture says, the splinter that is in Plato's eye while ignoring the beam that is in our own.

If, however, we consider philosophers and theologians as intelligent bodies, we notice not only what they said (already interpreted by translation), but also the particular circumstances in which they spoke. The circumstances in which a philosopher or theologian spoke are as important as *what he said*. For example, Socrates is re-

12. Ibid., 106e.
13. Plato, *Republic* VI. 509d.

ported to have uttered his "proof" of immortality shortly before his own death. His statement was not disinterested.

Like Socrates, Plotinus spoke most disparagingly of bodies in the last treatise he wrote before he died (*Ennead* 1.7), when he was afflicted with an illness so repulsive that his friends forsook him. "Death is a greater good," Plotinus said as he lay dying. "Life in a body is an evil in itself, but the soul comes into good . . . by not living the life of the compound but separating itself even now."[14] Like others, philosophers have social and physical experience that prompts and directs their thoughts! Lack of attention to the social and historical circumstances in which ideas were articulated results in the reification of those ideas. Thus it is important to examine ideas not only for their philosophical antecedents—their development as ideas—but also historically, in the actual lives of intelligent bodies. Philosophers should be, but seldom are, interpreted by historians.

Plato introduced a very valuable and useful concept. The "double ignorance," he said, occurs when a person does not know, and does not know that he does not know: "another form of thinking that one is wise when one is not . . . is to think that one knows what one does not know."[15] Plato's Socrates, unlike contemporary Sophist teachers, was distinguished simply by the fact that he *knew* that he did not know. Real ignorance occurs only when a person does not know, but *thinks that he does know.*[16]

14. Plotinus, *Ennead* 1.7.3.
15. Plato, *Republic* VI. 509d.
16. Plato, *Apology* 29a; *Laws* 9.963c.

We *know* so little, Socrates (Plato's protagonist) demonstrated again and again. Yet without hesitation we pronounce on such unknowns as others' motivation, the future, and what happens when we die. In fact, we often declare with great assurance that we *know* something we cannot possibly know, attempting to *make something true* (or at least *sound* true) by the robust vehemence of our declaration.

Plotinus articulated the difficulty of knowing even more clearly than did Plato. He acknowledged the inadequacy of *description* that, of necessity, requires inaccurate speech. One of his most frequently used expressions was *hoion* ("so to speak"), and he advised his hearers and readers to remember that he was forced to use language that did not adequately mirror reality, especially when he spoke of the Good or the One: "For this is how one has to speak of [the One] since one is unable to speak as one should."[17] Language *necessarily* distorts; it is a crude and fragile tool, but it's all we have.

Stoics

By the first centuries of the Common Era the question of how such disparate entities as matter and intelligence can be joined had become the *problem* of body and soul. Stoic philosophers analyzed three ways in which disparate entities can be united: "juxtaposition, as illustrated by heaps of wheat, barley, and lentils, or the pebbles and sand of the seashore"; mixture, a mutual extension of dis-

17. Plotinus, *Ennead* 6.8.18. See also my discussion of *hoion* in *Plotinus on Body and Beauty*, 27.

similar parts entering into one another at all points, as illustrated by water and wine (with "components at least theoretically resolvable into constituent parts"); and confusion, "corruption of all original distinctive qualities, . . . so that a third thing is generated."[18] The mode in which intellect (*logos*) and matter are combined in bodies is mixture: "components [are] at least theoretically resolvable into constituent parts." This evaluation of the mixture of soul and body prompted "the longing to differentiate the components of the human being [which] pervaded late Roman philosophy and religion."[19] The Romans had a horror of *mixtus*, best indicated by their name for the contents of the sewers under the city of Rome: *mixtus*.

In the *Philebus*, Plato warned that "any compound, whatever it be, that does not by some means or other exhibit measure and proportion, is the ruin both of its ingredients and, first and foremost, of itself"; what one is bound to get in such cases is no real mixture, but confusion, "*a miserable mass of unmixed messiness.*"[20]

Christians

From the second-century apologists to Augustine's massive, early fifth-century *City of God against the Pagans*, Christian authors allied themselves with contemporary philosophy—especially, in the early centuries of the Christian movement, with Stoicism and popular Platonism. It is understandable that a poorly under-

18. Miles, *Augustine on the Body,* 80–81.
19. Ibid.
20. Plato, *Philebus* 64d-e. My italics.

stood, illegal, and persecuted "new religion" sought to answer both moral and intellectual objections by aligning itself with ancient and honorable philosophies. Yet Christianity's self-identification with philosophy has had immense consequences. One of the most durable of classical philosophy's influences on Christianity was its concept of person.

Christianity is deeply invested both in distinguishing soul and body, spiritual and material, *and* in overcoming or transcending this division. Spirit and matter *must* remain separate in order to produce the *frisson* achieved in bringing each as close as possible to the other, yet without mutual contamination.[21] Matter and spirit cannot collapse into one another, becoming a "third thing," confusion. Cultural discomfort with *mixtus* informed Augustine's early failure to understand the incarnation of Christ, a *mixtus* of divinity and humanity. He could not understand how God could remain unsullied while sharing humanity's "coats of flesh."[22]

My 1977 doctoral dissertation examined Augustine's effort to rethink the classical understanding of the value

21. There are other suggestions within Christian tradition. For example, in Eastern Orthodoxy, the relationship between human and divine is thought of as a *connection* to be explored, not a chasm to be bridged. While Western theologians maintained an absolute separation between God and human (and punished those, like Meister Eckhart and Marguerite Porete, who seemed to blur that distinction), Eastern theologians' idea of relationship as connection allowed the possibility and reality of deification.

22. *Confessions* 7.19. See also Patricia Cox Miller's discussion of the urgency of simultaneously establishing the nonnegotiable difference of matter and the holy, and the perennial urge to bring them as close together as possible, yet without mixture or confusion (*Corporeal Imagination,* 9).

of body. He clearly found the classical stacked components model incompatible with, if not contradictory to, Christian doctrines of creation, incarnation, and the resurrection of body. He understood the problem.[23] But he found no satisfactory solution because he was unwilling to identify and jettison the "silent thought" that persons are composed of (at least) two "things," body and soul/mind.

Quite astonishingly (and confusingly), for anyone accustomed to Western rhetoric about persons as composed of hierarchically arranged parts, Christian faith simultaneously employed and denied this proto-dualism. We need only take seriously the logic of Christian *practices* in order to notice the existence of another rhetoric, a rhetoric in which a unity that cannot be analyzed into parts—an intelligent body—is presumed.[24] The following examples illustrate.

Fourth-century catechetical instruction included not only explanation of the faith, but also physical disciplines. Together, instruction and disciplines aimed at the creation of a Christian intelligent body. Catechetical instructions specify exercises to retrieve body from Satan's ownership to Christ's ownership.

> During the seven weeks preceding Easter, those enrolled for baptism were instructed for three hours every day on the essentials of the faith, the evils of pagan amusements, and sexual morality.

23. In fact, in the process of writing her doctoral dissertation on Augustine, Arendt herself may have recognized the problem she described in the epigraph to this chapter.

24. The assumptions underlying Christian practices are examined in detail in my book, *The Word Made Flesh*.

> They also underwent daily exorcisms; every siz-
> able church had several exorcists whose job was
> to "blow out" the demons from the body of the
> catechumen, reciting an ancient prayer: "Come
> out of him/her, accursed one." While this was
> done the person stood on harsh sackcloth or
> rough animal skin. A sermon by Theodore of
> Mopsuestia explained: "You stand on garments
> of sackcloth so that from the fact that your feet
> are pricked and stung by the roughness you may
> remember your old sins and show penitence and
> repentance."[25]

Why the interweaving of instruction and bodily disciplines? Usually interpreters understand instruction as addressing the mind or soul and physical exercises as addressing the body. Plato had written, "We should not exercise the body without the soul or the soul without the body, and thus they will be *on their guard against each other* and be healthy and well balanced."[26] This rationale reveals the assumption that the person consists of "parts" that, if not antagonistic, at least require careful distin-guishing and monitoring. On the intelligent body model of person, however, it is not that body's experience is transferable to mind, but that the intelligent body reacts directly.

William of Ockham's famous razor can help: Assumptions introduced to explain a thing must not be multiplied beyond necessity (*entia non sunt multiplican-da praeter necessitate*). Why assume two "things" when one—the intelligent body—provides the necessary and sufficient basis on which to understand catechetical tech-

25. Miles, *Word Made Flesh*, 78.
26. *Timaeus* 88c.

niques. *Both* instruction and physical disciplines address the intelligent body, the locus of Christian commitment. *The rational mind, artificially disconnected from body, is incapable of commitment of the whole person.*

Some Christian liturgies and practices emphasize the distinction of material and spiritual elements, as in eucharistic liturgies in which the material elements of bread and wine are brought to the altar to be united by the *epiclesis* in which the Spirit is invoked to function within the bread and wine. In the first accounts of baptism, on the other hand, adult catechumens were baptized naked in the full congregation after long preparation in which both instruction and ascetical practices readied the person for entrance into the Christian community.[27] Affirmed by catechetical training and the baptismal ritual, though not named as such, the intelligent body was both site and symbol of Christian commitment.

Concepts of "person" are inevitably "fleshed out" in social arrangements. Although most, if not all, Western societies could be discussed as exemplifying social arrangements that embody differing values associated with soul/mind and body, an ancient example will illustrate.

Slave Bodies

Due to a lack of slave writings, the subjectivity of slaves is inaccessible. The bodies of slaves popu-

27. Until Christianity became a tolerated religion of the Roman Empire, catechetical instruction was conducted one on one. After the fourth-century "Peace of the Church," when the large numbers of converts made personal instruction impossible, the forty-day period of Lent was designated for the preparation of candidates.

late the pages passed down to us from the centuries that witnessed the rise of Christianity. These same pages, however, yield little insight into how slaves understood themselves and their agency in the world. We know that slavery marked the body: through shaved heads, tattoos, fetters, and the visible scars of physical discipline. We do not know, however, how slavery marked the person who bore these stigmata.[28]

Body's low value had social as well as personal effects. The Greek word for body (*to sōma*) was used as a synonym for slave (*ho doulos*).[29] In her book *Slavery in Early Christianity*, Jennifer Glancy argues persuasively that the New Testament was written from the perspective of slaveholders. She questions the possibility that slaves could adopt Christianity on two grounds. First, patriarchs of households chose the religion of the extended household, including slaves. Second, early Christianity's sexual purity requirements excluded slaves because "slaveholders had unrestricted sexual access to their slaves." Glancy writes that "the bodies of slaves were [constantly] vulnerable to abuse and penetration."[30] It was legally impossible for a slave to be raped.[31] "All evidence suggests that the sexual use of female and young male slaves was widespread."[32] Augustine listed the most common objects of adult acquisitive grasping as no longer related to childhood's

28. Glancy, *Slavery in Early Christianity*, 29.

29. Ibid., 10. See also Richlin's discussion of the slave's body in "Cicero's Head," 193–94.

30. Glancy, *Slavery in Early Christianity*, 12.

31. Richlin, "Cicero's Head," 194.

32. Glancy, *Slavery in Early Christianity*, 23.

"footballs, nuts, and pet sparrows," but to "gold, estates, and slaves."[33]

Were Romans' slaves considered persons or possessions?[34] Ancient literature reveals ambivalence, often within the same author, on this question. The "only classical legal work to have come down to us in substantially its original form," Gaius's *Institutes*,[35] distinguished between free and unfree "persons," suggesting that slaves were persons. On the other hand, Gaius wrote, "Corporeal things are things which can be touched, such as land, a slave, a garment, gold, silver."[36] Whether a slave was considered a person or an object, slaves were *bodies*.

Ignoring the painful physical reality suffered by slaves, Christian authors used slavery as a metaphor for sin. Slavery was caused by sin; Augustine cited the slave (*servus*) as evidence: "The first cause of servitude, therefore, is sin, by which man was placed under man in a condition of bondage." Trivializing the physical suffering of slavery, he went on to say, "Clearly, it is a happier lot to be the slave of a man than of a lust . . . [and] humility is as profitable to those who serve, as pride is harmful to those who rule."[37] Regarding slavery as an inevitable social evil, he did not, however, advocate its eradication. In this Augustine was not alone; none of his contemporaries could imagine that society could be maintained without slavery. The fact of slavery is usually forgotten when we admire Greek and Roman societies.

33. Augustine, *Confessions* 1.19.
34. Richlin, "Cicero's Head," 194.
35. *Oxford Classical Dictionary*, 2nd ed., s.v. "Slavery," 453.
36. Richlin, "Cicero's Head," 193.
37. Augustine, *City of God* 19.15.

In late antiquity, punishment was meted out according to civil status. While slaves could be struck, branded, and otherwise harmed, "the citizen's body was almost automatically an immune body. . . . It was considered an outrage . . . for a citizen even to be hit with a cane."[38] Moreover, ancient authors assumed that torture, authorized and conducted by the state, was necessary for the maintenance of public order. Both Christian martyrdom and the self-discipline of asceticism had roots in classical assumptions about the uses of pain and suffering.

> Christianity was forged in the crucible of the late Roman penal system. Every martyrdom was a truth contest in which Roman government officials sought to demonstrate state power, and Christian believers, through their preternatural endurance, sought to demonstrate its futility. . . . [W]ith the cessation of official persecution the ascetic movement became the heir to the idea that truth is something to be demonstrated with the body.[39]

In sum, classical and late antique literature, both philosophical and theological, reveals the difficulty of explaining persons. A consensus developed from the pre-Socratics forward that defining human persons depended upon *describing* the interaction of two (or more) distinct components. Description led to imagining soul and body as distinguishable entities that would be separated not only at death (Socrates), but also during life (Plotinus). Plotinus taught that the work of separating soul from

38. Richlin, "Cicero's Head," 195.

39. Gleason, "Truth Contests and Walking Corpses," in Porter, *Constructions of the Classical Body*, 305.

body during life was necessary to prevent mutual contamination. The distinction of human components was so
strongly established by the first centuries of the Christian
era that, despite beliefs and practices that argue for the
integrity of the person, another rhetoric insisted on the
essential disparity of these components.

3

Descartes, Pascal, and the Intelligent Body

What we misapprehend, we cannot use.

—Thomas Traherne[1]

Cogito ergo sum

—Descartes

Descartes

Descartes' early modern articulation of person as separate components summarized and extended a long tradition of proposals about the relationship of body and mind. Moreover, philosophers before Descartes thought that definite separation of the "components" occurred only in death. During life, the philosopher's task was to identify with and exercise rationality as "practice for

1. Traherne, *Centuries* 4.16.

dying."[2] Descartes (d. 1650) took a giant step into a fully realized dualism. Dualism proposed that "reality is of two distinct and irreducible kinds," which Descartes named a thinking substance (*res cogitans*) and an extended substance (*res extensa*). Descartes understood body and soul, or rational mind, to be separate throughout life.[3] He wrote,

> Now from the mere fact that I know for certain that I exist and that I cannot see anything else that belongs necessarily to my nature or essence except that I am a thinking thing, I rightly conclude that my essence exists in this alone, *that I am a thinking thing, a substance whose whole nature or essence is to think*. While it is possible that I have a body which is very closely joined to me; nevertheless, since on the one hand I have a clear and distinct idea of myself as a person that thinks and is not extended, and on the other hand, I have a distinct idea of the body as a thing that is extended and *does not think*. It is certain that this I, that is to say, my soul, which makes me what I am, is entirely and truly distinct from my body, and can be or exist without it.[4]

For Descartes, body is "the location of pains, emotional disturbances, sensations of pressure, and the processes we call involuntary, such as heartbeat, breathing, digesting, and reflexes." To the body belongs "everything that can be done without thoughtful attention, such as walking, singing, or sleep-walking."[5]

2. Plato, *Phaedo* 80e.

3. A fuller discussion of Descartes' method can be found in my *Word Made Flesh*, 325ff.

4. Descartes, *Meditations* VI. My italics.

5. Miles, *Word Made Flesh,* 331.

Descartes spoke to a new audience; in order to be accessible to ordinary people, he wrote in French, not in Latin, the language in which scholars communicated with one another. Descartes respected the intelligence of ordinary people: "Differences in opinion," he wrote, "are not due to differences in intelligence, but merely to the fact that we use different approaches and consider different things."[6] He presented his ideas as a *method* by which his own reasoning could be replicated. The method he described is explicitly first-personal: "My aim here is not to teach the method that each person should follow in order to conduct his reason well, but solely to show in what way I have tried to conduct my own."[7] He claimed that his method was for the purpose of understanding "not *what can be known*, but what *I* can know."

Far from aiming at "objectivity," the "Father of Rationalism" considered personal interest a necessary component of rational inquiry:

> It seemed to me that I would find much more truth in the reasoning which each person makes about the matters which are of concern to him, and of which the outcome is likely to punish him soon after if he has made a mistake, than of those which a man of letters makes in his study, concerning speculations that lead to no result, and will have no other consequences for him, except perhaps that he will be all the more vain about them the further they are from common sense.[8]

6. Descartes, *Discourse* 1.2.
7. Ibid., 1.4.
8. Ibid., 1.6.9–10.

Descartes' analysis carried the day. After him Leibniz described the "two distinct and irreducible kinds" as actual and possible worlds; Kant called "them" nominal and phenomenal worlds.

Perhaps prompted by the objections that arose as soon as he published *Discourse on the Method* (1637), Descartes' *Meditations* (1641) nervously interrogates the separation of body and soul he has proposed: "Nature also teaches me by these sensations of pain, hunger, thirst, etc., that I am not only lodged in my body as a pilot in a vessel, but that I am very closely united to it, and so to speak so closely intermingled with it that I seem to compose with it one whole." Nevertheless, he concluded that "all these sensations of hunger, thirst, pain, etc., are in truth none other than confused modes of thought which are produced by the union and *apparent intermingling* of mind and body. . . . The mind or soul of man is entirely different from the body."[9]

Along with Descartes' insistence that mind and body are separate entities came a high valuation of mind. It was no accident that his identification of mind and its activity, reason, as the essential person occurred in the seventeenth century when historical circumstances created the conditions in which his proposal had appeal and came to have consensus despite the initial objections of philosophers and theologians. The West was experiencing devastating wars of religion resulting from the sixteenth-century reformations. Approximately three-fifths of Germany's sixteen million people were killed in the Thirty Years' War (1618–1648) involving Germany,

9. Descartes, *Meditations* VI. My italics.

Bohemia, Poland, Denmark, Sweden, Switzerland, and France. The Peace of Westphalia ended the war by stipulating that populations must adhere to the religious preference of rulers, whether Catholicism, Calvinism, or Lutheranism. But religious persecution did not cease. Persecution of Protestants (Huguenots) in France resulted in the slaughter of thousands and the emigration of 250,000 Protestants. Anabaptists, with their presumed disloyalty to nation-states, were excluded from the Peace and suffered heavy persecution. The persecution of suspected witches in Europe and New England also led to the execution of many women and men in the seventeenth century; scholars' estimates vary wildly as to actual numbers.

Clyde Manschreck describes well the conditions that prompted the success of rationalism:

> It was as if people were saturated with religion, with the intolerance, persecution, and strife that accompanied it, weary of fanatical dogmas, witch-burning, heretic hunting, inquisitional racks, and wholesale slaughter. The authoritative claims of the Roman Catholic Church had been broken, and the equally dogmatic claims of the Protestants seemed to have no more authoritative substantiation than those of Roman orthodoxy. Advocates on both sides put their opponents to death, each side claiming finality for its point of view. But people had grown weary.[10]

In these circumstances, the hope that reason could reduce violence was attractive.

10. Manshreck, *Melanchthon*, 276.

Pascal

> The heart has its reasons of which
> reason knows nothing.[11]

Pascal (d. 1662), Descartes' contemporary and compatriot, understood human beings quite differently. He described a powerful formative experience on a scrap of paper found, after he died, sewn into his clothing.

> From about half-past ten in the evening until half-past midnight: FIRE. God of Abraham, God of Isaac, God of Jacob, not of the philosophers and scholars. Certainty, certainty, heartfelt joy, peace. The world forgotten, and everything except God. Joy, joy, joy, tears of joy . . . Jesus Christ, Jesus Christ . . .[12]

Pascal's experience left him in no doubt; he was uninterested in rational arguments to prove or justify Christianity. The energy and urgency of his *Pensées* (*Thoughts*) is very different from the reasoning of his slightly older contemporary. For Pascal, neither intellect nor physical existence provided certainty and stability.

> What sort of freak, then, is human being? How novel, how monstrous, how chaotic, how prodigious! Judge of all things; feeble earthworm; repository of truth; sink of doubt and error; glory and refuse of the universe.[13]

11. Pascal, *Pensées* #423.
12. Pascal, #309.
13. Ibid., #131.

He proposed the following image of the human situation:

> Imagine a number of men in chains, all under sentence of death, some of whom are each day butchered in the sight of the others; those remaining see their own condition in that of their fellows, and looking at each other with grief and despair await their turn. This is an image of the human condition.[14]

Pascal noticed the paradox of humans in the universe:

> A human being is only a reed, the weakest in nature, but he is a thinking reed. There is no need for the whole universe to take up arms to crush him; a vapor, a drop of water, is enough to kill him. But even if the universe were to crush him, he would still be nobler than his slayer, because he knows that he is dying, and the advantage that the universe has over him. The universe knows none of this.[15]

Pascal admired mind, but primarily for its awareness of death. Mind, however, lacks the ability to understand the most important aspects of human existence: it lacks self-knowledge; it cannot find God; and it is governed inevitably by perspective. "All our reasoning," Pascal said, "comes down to surrendering to feeling. . . . Reason is available but can be bent in any direction."[16]

Despite humans' physical frailty and mental disorientation, Pascal said, we long for happiness:

14. Ibid., #434.
15. Ibid., #200.
16. Ibid., #530.

> All people seek happiness. There are no excep-
> tions. However different the means they may
> employ, they all strive toward this goal. The
> reason why some go to war and some do not is
> the same desire in both, but interpreted in two
> different ways. The will never takes the least step
> except to that end. This is the motive of every
> act of every person, including those who go and
> hang themselves.[17]

Pascal's famous wager was his answer to Descartes. Reason cannot prove God; thus, he said, religion must appeal to humans' self-interest: "Weigh the gain and the loss, in betting . . . that God is. If you win, you win all; if you lose, you lose nothing. Bet, therefore, that God is, without hesitating."[18] Pascal disclaimed the implied frivolity of the wager by insisting that the *practice* of Christian life—practicing the liturgical habits and moral requirements of a Christian community—provides the most compelling proof of the truth of Christianity: "Habit provides the strongest proofs and those that are most believed."[19] Invoking the ancient Stoic admonition to act as if you are virtuous, and by acting as if you are virtuous, you imperceptibly become virtuous, he even advised going through the motions in order to experience the quality of Christian life. Practice precedes and produces belief.[20]

17. Ibid., #148.
18. Ibid., #418.
19. Ibid., #821.
20. Miles, *Word Made Flesh,* 338.

Rationalism and Pietism

Two seventeenth-century movements, emerging from the Wars of Religion, transcended national boundaries. The attraction of both of these movements must be seen in the context of their historical circumstances. Rationalism, initiated by Descartes, identified the person with his capacity for reason, a reaction to the extremes of religion. Pietism, like Pascal (but without direct reference to Pascal), located religious conviction firmly in the individual heart. Pietism focused on "the heart strangely warmed," as John Wesley described his experience of conversion. John Wesley's brother, Charles, wrote hymns that repetitiously insist that it is the individual who is the recipient of salvation ("He died for *me*"), not a national church chosen by the ruler of the territory. One effect of the focus on *individual* conversion was that it began to preclude state-sponsored persecution of those of other persuasions.

Wesley was often unwelcome in churches, so he began to preach wherever and whenever he could.

> A large congregation was present at five [A.M.] and stood unmoved, notwithstanding some heavy showers. . . . The roads were so extremely slippery, it was with much difficulty that we reached Bedford. We had a pretty large congregation; but the stench from the swine under the Room was scarce supportable. Was ever a preaching place over a hog-sty before?[21]

Descartes' identification of the self with mind may seem to be incompatible with Pietism's religion of the

21. Wesley, *Journal*, 134, 144.

heart; yet both shared common values arising from a common European culture. Their differences should not be exaggerated. The fundamentally religious foundation of *The Discourse on the Method of Rightly Conducting the Reason* is evident in Descartes' preoccupation with securing a God who could neither be doubted nor imagined to be a deceiver. And, as has been discussed, truth was as personal for Descartes as religion was for Pascal and the Pietists. John Wesley's sermons, preached in the fields at 6:00 A.M. to thousands of people, were not revival preaching by later standards. They were long, closely reasoned expositions of doctrine. Reason was valued highly by Pietists.

Nevertheless, one effect of Descartes' appropriation of "God" as a rational principle was decisively to split religion and theology. Before the seventeenth century, "belief" had joined religious feeling and intellectual conviction; but Descartes' method of doubt effectively separated them. Could beliefs be doubted? Certainly. The first moment of his method jettisoned "what is not clearly known." How could anyone claim to *know* what could only be strongly *felt*?[22] After the initial moment of doubt, Descartes' tortuous arguments built the first logical argument claiming to guarantee God's existence.

Turning Over the "Components"

Fast forward to the twentieth century. Contemporary neurophysiologists object to the Cartesian analysis of the

22. In support of doubt, he might have invoked Plato's "double ignorance" (in which one does not *know*, but does not know that he does not *know*).

human person as *cogito ergo sum*. Turning the traditional idea of "person" upside down, they place body in the commanding position; mind receives orders from body.[23]

Antonio Damasio argues that "body and brain are integrated by mutually targeted biochemical and neural circuits."[24] Even "self," he says, "is a very complex bodily feeling: the part of the mind we call self [is], biologically speaking, grounded on a collection of non-conscious neural patterns standing for the part of the organism we call body." He writes of "the body behind the self."[25] In short, "there is no thinking that is independent of the feedback mechanism linking sensory input, body chemistry, the body map, and neural activity."[26] "The physical foundation is not recognized," Damasio writes, because "mind produces a screen that hides the body."[27]

For contemporary neurophysiologists, mind is an epiphenomenon of body. Yet it has seemed abundantly clear to historical philosophers and theologians that rational mind must rule the ensemble. However, all seem to agree, despite their different organization of parts, that persons are two things. Contemporary philosopher Maxine Sheets Johnstone argues that persons cannot be dissected and analyzed into parts.

Sheets-Johnstone proposes a model of person that she calls the "first-person body" or the "intelligent body." According to this model, "person" is neither an epiphenomenon of mind nor a body that makes of the

23. Damasio, *Feeling of What Happens*, 41.
24. Ibid., 87.
25. Ibid., 133.
26. Smail, *On Deep History and the Brain*, 145.
27. Damasio, *Feeling of What Happens*, 28.

brain a "captive audience." The first-person body, Sheets-Johnstone writes,

> is the body that we know directly in the context or process of being alive. It is the body with which we came into the world prior to technology or science telling us what we are made of, how we are put together, how that togetherness works. The body that emerges from the womb alive and kicking is the primordial one. From the moment of birth that body is the center and origin of our being in the world. It is, in fact, our first world and reality. The first-person body is not a body that we outgrow, or even can outgrow; it is only one we can choose to deny or deprecate. It is a body not lacking biological reality, but a body whose biological reality is neither separable from nor a third-person dimension of its lived and living presence.[28]

According to Sheets-Johnstone, when we analyze a human being according to components, *no matter how we stack the components, we have already lost the person.* According to this model it is not simply that mind/soul and body are inseparable, but that "they" do not exist.[29] Our ancient habit of thinking of the person as assembled from components and dissectible into those components makes it very difficult for us to think of the whole person.

How, then, was the separation of body and soul/mind rendered plausible, much less persuasive, and finally, unquestionable? Sheets-Johnstone answers this question by identifying two aspects of body, the lived body (described above) and the visible body: "It is the visual body that

28. Sheets-Johnstone, *Corporeal Turn*, 20.
29. Ibid.

came to be abstracted from the lived body and to stand out from it as a distinctly physical entity."[30] "The visual body in time came to be seen as an outsider, a thing out there, a materiality," an "object among objects."[31] Vision, "queen of the senses," became the arbiter of reality: seeing is believing. And rationality, "the eye of the mind," with its tool, logical argument, supported and explained the unseen.

Part One has sketched the development of the "silent thought" about what a person *is* from pre-Socratic philosophers to the recent proposals of neurophysiologists and of a philosopher/evolutionary biologist, Sheets-Johnstone. I have endeavored to uncover the problems—historical and contemporary—inherent in assuming that persons are built of components, but also to make several suggestions about why we stubbornly cling to the hierarchically arranged components model. I have proposed that Sheets-Johnstone's description of "person" as intelligent body accounts for human experience more adequately than does the components model. But the latter is very deeply entrenched in our psyches, so much so that even authors whose evident model is the intelligent body often claim adherence to body and soul/mind when attempting to explain persons.

How can we get from the traditional model to the intelligent body? Plotinus and Augustine were impatient with imagining a goal but providing no instructions or energy for getting there. In Part Two, I explore some suggestions about how we might *think differently* and therefore *experience differently* if we conceptualize persons as

30. Ibid., 103.
31. Ibid, 100ff.

42

intelligent bodies. My suggestions for *getting to* a more fruitful model of person than the components model are first-personal. I have come upon them by chance in the pursuit of other interests. Again, they do not constitute an argument, but by them I hope to stimulate further exploration for answers to the ancient question, how should we live? Richard Rorty made the following observation:

> The only thing that can displace an intellectual world is another intellectual world—a new alternative, rather than an argument against an old alternative. . . . I do not think that demonstrations of "internal incoherence" or of "presuppositional relationships" ever do much to disabuse us of bad old ideas or institutions. Disabusing gets done, instead, by offering us sparkling new ideas or utopian visions of glorious new institutions. The result of genuinely original thought . . . is not so much to refute or subvert our previous beliefs as to help us forget them by giving us a substitute for them.[32]

In brief, Part One offers a historical and philosophical sketch of the construction of person. Part Two proposes some practical suggestions ("sparkling new ideas or utopian visions") for imagining the intelligent body.

32. Rorty, "Is Derrida a Transcendental Philosopher?" 208–9.

PART TWO

The Life of Intelligent Bodies

4

Intelligent Bodies Move

It is the curse of theology always to forget that
God is love, that is, movement.

—GERARDUS VAN DER LEEUW[1]

In the beginning is—and was—movement, sheer
movement.

—MAXINE SHEETS-JOHNSTONE[2]

Maxine Sheets-Johnstone's essay "Thinking in Movement" argues that thinking is not "an exclusively mental event"; rather, thinking in movement is "a way of being in the world."[3] "Thinking itself . . . is a form of animation: moving forward, backward, quickly, slowly, narrowly, broadly, lightly, ponderously, [thinking] itself

---

1. Van der Leeuw, *Sacred and Profane Beauty*, 74.
2. Sheets-Johnstone, *Corporeal Turn*, 60.
3. Ibid., 35.

is kinetic."[4] Sheets-Johnstone begins with the observation that the infant's "initial concepts are linked to dynamic events, to kinetic experiences both of its own movement and movement in its surrounding world . . . [so that] rather than designating the period before language as *pre-linguistic*, we should speak of the advent of language as *post-kinetic*."[5] Further, "An infant's first mode of thinking is in movement."[6]

Two assumptions hinder a broader understanding of the activity of thinking: First, the assumption that thinking requires, and always occurs within, language; second, "that thinking and language are tied in an exclusive way to rationality."[7] If all thinking is not done with something we artificially isolate from body and call rational mind, then thinking, rationality, even logic are properties of an intelligent body. Infants understand by moving. An infant does not decide, "Okay, now I'm going to roll over"—or sit up, or walk. Indeed, "infants have nonlinguistic concepts . . . in advance of language. . . . [They] begin to understand gravity and inertia by the time they are six months old."[8] In short,

> there is a richly subtle nonverbal world that is there from the beginning of each of our lives, a dynamic world that is neither mediated by language nor a stepping stone to language . . . a dynamic world articulating intercorporeal intentions that, although clearly affective in origin,

4. Ibid., 60–61.
5. Ibid., 5.
6. Ibid., 48.
7. Ibid., 36.
8. Ibid., 42–43.

are enmeshed in "agentivity," in expectations, in consequential relationships, and thereby in the phenomenon of thinking in movement.[9]

Moreover, thinking in movement is "transmitted with greater speed than a verbal message." Sheets-Johnstone quotes infant psychiatrist Daniel Stern: "Language is slow. . . . It breaks apart rich, complicated global experiences into relatively impoverished component parts." For the young child, language "creates a wide gulf between [a] familiar nonverbal world of experience and [a] new world of words," a schism that is "confusing and at times painful."[10] Sheets-Johnstone concludes, "Thinking in movement is our primary way of making sense of the world, . . . a capacity that does not diminish with age, but merely becomes submerged or hidden by the capacity and practice of thinking in words."[11]

Docile Bodies

The alternative to intelligent bodies that live, move, discover, and learn is docile bodies. Michel Foucault described the constriction of movement Western societies routinely require of citizens. From students to captains of industry, most of those who succeed sit quietly at desks for many hours every day. "Docile bodies" are bodies that are "manipulated, shaped, trained . . . [A docile body] obeys, responds, becomes skillful, and increases its forces . . . [it] may be subjected, used, transformed and

9. Ibid., 48.
10. Ibid.
11. Ibid., 43.

improved." Why do people accept the strictures of a docile body? Bodies tolerate conditioning to docility because they enjoy the considerable pleasures of learning new skills and achieving the rewards of power through knowledge, in exchange for the body's domination and control at the level of "movements, gestures, attitudes, rapidity."[12]

There is no single authority that demands docile bodies; rather, the demand accrues from myriad locations within and to the depths of societies. But it is important to note that "power operate[s] not only as a coercive force, but also—and simultaneously—as a mechanism of attraction."[13] In fact, attraction is ultimately more powerful than coercion because coercion fosters rebellion. Rather, attraction and coercion act in concert and simultaneously to form a strong incentive to look and behave in ways that serve the political and economic forces active in societies.[14]

To illustrate his point, Foucault analyzed the minutely detailed training that transformed eighteenth-century peasants into soldiers, that "produce[d] subjected and practiced bodies, 'docile' bodies."[15] Peasants were made into soldiers by disciplines in which "posture is gradually corrected [and] a calculated restraint runs slowly through each part of the body, mastering it, making it pliable, ready at all times, turning silently into the automism of habit." Minute attention to detail is required; no feature

---

12. Foucault, *Discipline and Punish*, 155.

13. Foucault, *Reader*, 324.

14. Ibid.

15. Ibid., 138.

of posture, gesture, or uniform is too small to contribute to "the mastery of each individual over his own body."[16]

> Recruits become accustomed to "holding their heads high and erect; to standing upright, without bending the back, to sticking out the belly, throwing out the chest and throwing back the shoulders; and, to help them acquire the habit, they are given the position while standing against a wall in such a way that the heels, the thighs, the waist, and the shoulders touch it."[17]

Docile bodies are shaped in societies according to gender roles and expectations. There are particular configurations for women: "they are squeezed, patterned, molded, and formed by the social pathologies of constructs like beauty, aura, presence."[18]

In her book *Female Sexualization: A Collective Work of Memory*, German feminist Frigga Haug and her collective explored in detail the production of femininity in and on the late twentieth-century German female body. In their "memory work," Haug and her associates came to understand that female socialization is simultaneously a *sexualization* of a woman's body and a subjectification, a "process by which individuals work themselves into social structures they themselves do not consciously determine."[19] Remembering "the laborious efforts of our educators to drill us not only in washing, teeth-cleaning,

16. Ibid., 137.

17. Ibid., 179–80. Here Foucault quotes from the "Ordinance of 20 March 1764."

18. Pfister, *Staging Depth*, 203, quoted by Becker, *Myth of Empowerment*, 94.

19. Haug, *Female Sexualization*, 59.

hygiene, but also in posture, the proper position of the arms and legs, the proper position of the mouth," participants reconstructed the coaching by which they were to embody their expected role in their society.[20] Their memories are a painstaking account of female socialization/sexualization, specific to their time and location, but with significant similarity to the experiences of women in other Western industrial societies at the end of the twentieth century. Each participant had stories about her own experiences, conversations, and the advice of family, schoolmates, and educators. These processes sexualized hair, body parts, especially legs (too long? too short?) but also breasts (too large? too small?) and stomach, clothing, movement, and facial expressions. The *"constant requirement to arouse desire"* revealed male ownership of the project. Yet members also recognized the fact of their own collaboration in the process, a collaboration grounded in the pleasure of learning the intricate and demanding skills of effectively inserting oneself into one's society. Pleasure and (more or less subtle) coercion must be perfectly balanced, creating a powerful attraction to owning the approved body.[21] Their goal in remembering and rehearsing their experiences, wrote Haug, "was to reach a point at which we no longer see ourselves through the eyes of others."[22]

20. Ibid., 30.

21. My book *Carnal Knowing: Female Nakedness and Religious Meaning in the Christian West* describes the pairing of images of female beauty and female ugliness in order to instruct what constitutes beauty, for which women should strive, and ugliness, which they should shun; Miles, *Carnal Knowing*, 145ff.

22. Haug, *Female Sexualization*, 39.

Haug and her interlocutors sought not only to identify and understand the intricate and detailed training by which female sexualization occurs, but also, and more importantly, how to break the domination of the socially constructed docile female body. They recognized that it is unlikely that an individual can effectively rebel. "We aim," they wrote, "to develop ways of living collectively, and thus to escape individual isolation."[23]

Most of Haug's memory work consists of examining how women in late twentieth-century German culture were instructed in the grooming and display of their bodies, but a brief section, "Notes on Women's Gymnastics," discusses the different display of men's and women's bodies promoted in gymnastics. Women gymnasts, she writes, are encouraged to "make their bodies more malleable than men's." Haug sees their movements as "gestures of submission." Among men, by contrast, "strength is put on display."[24] "Strength is not rejected by the women's leaders, only visible strength."[25] A member of the women's team leadership described the ideal of women's gymnastics:

> The character of women's gymnastics is demonstrated by the greater diversity of its forms and most particularly by the uniquely feminine quality of movements which are lighter and looser, which flow more rhythmically than those of men, making even the most difficult exercises appear as joyful play.[26]

23. Ibid., 282.
24. Ibid., 176.
25. Ibid., 178.
26. Ibid.

The docile body is controlled by rationality—not usually by the individual's chosen purpose, but by mechanisms of power. It is the soldier's body, willing to march, kill, and huddle in trenches overrun by rats; it is the student's body, willing to sit for hours every day in uncomfortable chairs, listening or reading.[27] It is the woman's body, discussed by Haug and her collective, who write about the subtle coercion involved in the *pleasure* of learning how to control and train one's body. It is the financially successful body of late capitalism.[28]

Improvisational Dance

The intelligent body thinks in movement. Dance improvisation is Sheets-Johnstone's paradigm of the experience of thinking in movement, a conversation between intelligent bodies, bodies that know what to do and in which there is no "mind-doing" that is separate from "body-doing."[29] Dancer/philosopher Kimerer LaMothe describes watching a video of her own performance in which, although carefully choreographed, everything did not go as planned:

27. Each spring, daylight savings time will forfeit an hour, reverting to Pacific Standard Time. In the fall, daylight savings time will resume, encouraging people by earlier light to get to work on time. American society requires that its citizens work and rewards them for overwork so that they earn money with which to purchase the commodities whose sales maintain the economy.

28. Hennessy, *Profit and Pleasure*, 74ff.

29. *Corporeal Turn*, 32. Sheets-Johnstone's interdisciplinary publications no doubt required many hours, days, months, and years of stationary study. But she is also a dancer, and she writes about the *experience*, not the theory, of dance.

> I watch the video of the Saturday performance
> and I see. Every time my mind froze with fear
> at some unexpected occurrence, my bodily self
> responded by creating something new that was
> in itself beautiful, and sometimes, even more
> beautiful than what I had planned. *It was as
> if my bodily self knew what to do.* In the hours
> of practice and attention, cultivating a sensory
> awareness of the movement making me, I had
> created and become patterns of sensing and
> responding that had guided me smoothly and
> steadily through the challenges at hand.[30]

LaMothe describes with precision the movement of her intelligent body. However, she still works within mind-body language. Her "mind froze," but her "bodily self" knew what to do. Language does not help us communicate (to ourselves and others) that we are not *two things*, a mind that freezes and a body that "knows what to do." We are *one thing*, a body with intelligence, a body that knows how to be aware and to respond, a mind-full body. LaMothe's expression "bodily self" attempts to express this concept, but retains the possibility of splitting off into components. Moreover, "bodily self" does not explicitly acknowledge body's cognition and *intelligence*. In fact, it was LaMothe's intelligent body that felt fright and quickly responded to address that fear.

All movement is dance, not only choreographed or improvisational dance. Even the smallest movements are, in essence, dance. Breathing is dance: During the reformations of the sixteenth century, congregational hymn-singing was recognized to be a strong form of community

---

30. LaMothe, *Family Planting*, 207. My italics.

building. People who sing together breathe together, and breathing together, they bond together.

Three Stories about Movement

My first hospice patient—I'll call her Evelyn—had breast cancer and dementia. Evelyn's apartment was filled with beautiful artworks she had executed, mostly paintings, collages, and weavings. I thought that I would relate to her through our mutual interest in art. But, beyond telling me about her training in all kinds of techniques and media, she did not want to talk about art. She talked about teaching art at the Jewish Community Center, telling me at least twenty times in an afternoon that her students would come in saying, "I'm not going to be able to do this, Mrs. G." And she would tell them, "Oh yes you can." "And they *could*," she always concluded triumphantly.

At first it seemed impossible to sit with her for four hours at a time; her mental soundtrack repeated the same stories over and over, accompanied by the same gestures. After the first afternoon, I was exhausted, and Evelyn's husband—I'll call him John—as he walked me to the elevator, said, "Will you be able to stand this?" I reflected that *he* "stood it" twenty-four hours a day and I answered that of course I could stand it for four hours a week. Gradually I found that I could distract Evelyn a little from the ruts of her memory. I could get her talking about London during the war, about being brought by ship to the United States along with hundreds of other war brides, about her garden in Los Angeles.

We both loved to listen to classical music. Her mother was a violinist who practiced through thick and thin, including during the Battle of Britain, telling her children "shhh" (a gesture Evelyn repeated) while she practiced. "She still practices," Evelyn insisted. When John returned she asked him how old her mother was now ("John will know!"). John quietly replied, "She is no longer with us."

One day Evelyn started gently conducting the music as we listened. I did, too, and gradually we conducted it more and more wildly, dancing while sitting down, laughing. She said to me, "None of my other friends will listen to music with me." And, of course, under most circumstances, one doesn't visit a friend in order to listen to recorded music. The proximity of death often frees both the "dying" person and her visitor to a broader palette of activities than customary social behavior. I found that hospice patients are less attached to a self-image than are most of us. They are often eager to play, to move, even if only to conduct a symphony while sitting in a chair; they like to have fun. When language recedes, they often express themselves in movement.

When I was teaching I sometimes noticed bruises on the outside of my thighs that puzzled me. Finally I realized that I got them from bumping into my desk as I walked around it, distracted, not feeling the bruises as they occurred. My office was large enough that I could easily walk around my desk without bumping into it, so I realized that I was simply moving at the wrong pace, unaware of my body in relation to objects in the room. If I paid attention to moving more gracefully, I thought, I wouldn't have to have a car accident to get my attention.

In a telecast of the 2008 Olympic games, gold medal–winning gymnast Shawn Johnson was shown walking to a chair in the warm-up area of the stadium, unaware that the camera was on her. Suddenly she gave a little jump and did a double somersault in the air. I can only imagine what this movement *felt* like; it *looked* like energy and delight, pure exuberance expressed with her whole body, so beautiful.

It is not easy to refuse the docile body of gender socialization in late capitalist society. Recently I heard, on good authority, that if a person exercises vigorously every day and then sits at work for the rest of the day, the health benefits of the exercise are cancelled by the hours of sitting.[31] Moreover, few Americans can avoid long periods of driving in which we are exposed not only to traffic accidents but also to myriad physical problems caused by simultaneous inertia and tension. The foods we eat and the air we breathe contain their own dangers. The stores and offices we patronize bombard our ears with sounds that are both trivial and distracting. American public culture creates environments that challenge and discourage intelligent bodies. Little time or space is provided in which to think about what we are seeing, hearing, and experiencing. Our movements are constrained by crowded streets and public transportation. In order to breathe fresh air, see nature, or hear music that transports us, we must plan to leave our ordinary surroundings and move, temporarily, to other spaces. It is difficult to find the leisure to experience the large rhythm—movement—of the

31. It is somewhat reassuring, however, to learn that the simple act of standing for a couple of minutes every two hours restores the health benefits of one's exercise.

ocean. When we make nourishing leisure a priority, we are healed; we promise ourselves that we will take time out more frequently. Then we get to work, and because Western culture supports work rather than leisure, we forget.

5

Intelligent Bodies Feel

The heart within me is not of iron, but pitiful,
even as thine.
—THE ODYSSEY

In this chapter I consider attitudes toward feeling in several different historical contexts. My example of widely
differing cultural interpretations of feeling is suffering.
Nothing might seem, at first glance, more "natural" than
suffering, but as my examples show, in actuality, few experiences are more susceptible to widely different interpretations. An *experience* of suffering strongly depends
on the meaning invested in it by culture and community.

Two kinds of feeling that had negative meaning in
classical culture were valued highly in early Christianity:
suffering and compassion. The two are related; greater
value attached to suffering prompts greater compassion
for the sufferer.

Suffering

Pain is often thrust upon us in this life, but
suffering is voluntary.[1]

In *The Body in Pain: The Making and Unmaking of the
World*, Elaine Scarry claims that "pain destroys not only
personal capacities, but social meaning as well."[2] In her
analysis, pain is unsharable, world-destroying, and resis-
tant to language; thus, it dissolves essential social connec-
tions. Pain is destructive precisely because it is so hard to
put "the experience into words. . . . Pain shatters the con-
nections between body and voice, separates who we are
into near meaningless components, and thus fragments
our personal integrity."[3] Like Scarry, classical authors saw
nothing but passivity and abjection in suffering; suffering
was simply something that happened to a person.

Christine Mohrmann has studied dramatic changes
in the usage of several words from classical to Christian
Latin. In classical Latin *patior* denoted weakness and abjection. In Christian Latin the pejorative sense of *patior*
disappeared;[4] it became an honorific word. Suffering, the
stone that the (classical) builders rejected, became the
cornerstone of Christianity.[5]

Early Christian literature reveals a different analysis
of the meaning and value of suffering; suffering was con-

1. Trott, *Holy Man's Journey*, 73.

2. Scarry, *Body in Pain*, 13.

3. Vance, "Medical Ethics," 12.

4. Mohrmann, *Etudes sur le latin des chrétiens*, 17.

5. *Enantiadromia* means conversion to its opposite, from suffering as abjection to suffering as salvific.

sidered an opportunity to achieve both selfhood and community.[6] Ignatius was the first Christian writer to use the Greek word *pathos* (suffering) to describe Christ's death; Christ's salvific suffering and death decisively altered the meaning and value of suffering for Christians.[7] "Christ's suffering was his essential message, and Christians' acceptance of suffering was the sign of their commitment to his message."[8] For Christians of the early centuries, suffering was not only "self-fashioning"; community was also established by suffering.

Early Christian *actae* (martyrdom accounts) contest Scarry's interpretation of pain as utterly destructive of self, community, and world.[9] In fact, precisely the opposite is described: Perpetua, awaiting martyrdom in prison, is reported as saying, "I am a Christian and I identify with the authority of my name." Perpetua identified with Christ's suffering, not by an act of the imagination, but with her actual suffering flesh. Her *acta* describes her approachinng martyrdom "with shining face and calm step as the wife of Christ and the beloved of God."[10]

Narrations of martyrs' actions during their torture and execution vividly picture the scene, stimulating readers' empathic identification with the martyr's pain. Perpetua's hagiographer reports that after being tossed by a mad heifer, she rearranged her tunic in order to cover her thighs, "thinking more of her modesty than of her

6. Perkins, *Suffering Self*, 189–90.

7. Regarding "pain as beneficial, and as a channel for encountering the divine" was not unique to Christianity; see ibid., 189.

8. Ibid.

9. Ibid., 104–5.

10. Miles, *Carnal Knowing*, 60–61.

pain." She also fastened her disheveled hair "for it was not right that a martyr should die with her hair in disorder, lest she might seem to be mourning in her hour of triumph."[11] More than the socialization of women readers is attempted in this account of "good grooming" for women martyrs. Graphic details place readers who were not present *at* the scene *within* the scene, encouraging their empathy.[12] The assumption of early Christian *actae* is that pain *is sharable*, either by the literal sharing of Christ's pain in martyrdom, or by compassionate feeling.

Moreover, confessors (Christians who were condemned, incarcerated, and awaiting execution) adjudicated arguments among fellow Christians, and even had the (contested) power to forgive sins, usually the prerogative of ordained clergy. It was pain—both the present pain of incarceration and the anticipated pain of execution—that conferred the confessors' self-definition and their power in the Christian community. Far from stripping away "world, self, and voice," pain and the anticipation of pain gave martyrs authorization and authority. Their *experience* (according to their hagiographers) was one of empowerment and joy.

11. Ibid., 61.

12. Ariel Glucklich's book *Sacred Pain* also disagrees with Scarry's assertion that pain eludes language and thus is incommunicable. Referring to ascetic practices, he writes, "Religious individuals have hurt themselves because the pain they produced was meaningful and is not only subject to verbal communication but also figures in our ability to empathize and share" (xii).

Glucklich's consistent use of the language of "body and soul" assumes the traditional construction of persons as components, as "parts." His subtitle (*Hurting the Body for the Sake of the Soul*) imagines a dualism that is more adequately explained by imagining the person as an intelligent body, simultaneously experiencing and interpreting pain.

Scarry does not discuss Christian martyrdom; to do so would have seriously challenged her thesis. The dramatic conflict of interpretations I have discussed demonstrates that pain is ambiguous; the *experience* of pain is highly susceptible to personal and social interpretation. In the early Christian situation in which local or Empire-wide martyrdoms occurred approximately once in every generation, "Christian discourse [redefined] some of the most basic signifiers of any culture—the body, pain, and death."[13]

After the Peace of the Church in the early fourth century, when martyrdoms ceased in the western Roman Empire, martyrdom continued to inform the festivals, liturgies, hymns, and images of the Christian churches. Christians were encouraged imaginatively to meditate on and identify with Christ's sufferings. Moreover, the seventh-century text *Barlaam and Joasaph* makes explicit the connection between martyrdom and asceticism, the "daily martyrdom": Asceticism "arose from men's desire to become martyrs in will that they might not miss the glory of them who were made perfect by blood."[14]

Most people, whether Christian or not, are likely to name the crucifixion as the central image of Christianity. Whether presented as a triumph, as in Eastern Orthodox icons in which Christ reigns from the cross, or in images that emphasize the terrible physicality of his suffering (such as the *Isenheim Altarpiece*), crucifixion scenes appear in most Christian churches. Habituated to this scene of violence, most Christians do not notice its horror.

13. Perkins, *Suffering Self*, 115.
14. *St. John Damascene: Barlaam and Joasaph.*

In the early centuries of the Common Era, the threat and reality of martyrdom created a focus on suffering that is presently ignored. Twenty-first-century Christianity has lost the ancient and centuries-long emphasis on sharing Christ's suffering as Christ shares the believer's suffering.[15] In post-Freudian contemporary Western societies, suffering is not considered triumphal, and I do not urge that suffering be reappropriated as a Christian value. Nevertheless, twenty-first-century Christians should recognize that in rejecting suffering (whenever possible), we are more like the neighbors of early Christians than like early Christians themselves. We should also recognize that many Christians outside the West still suffer persecution for their Christian confession.

Compassion

We share each other's experiences when we suffer with others from seeing their pain and feel happy and relaxed [with others] and are naturally drawn to love them: for without a sharing of experience there could not be love.

—PLOTINUS[16]

Coliseum audiences sometimes felt compassion for the animals brought to Rome to fight and suffer for their en-

15. Traveling in Japan I noticed that there were few representations of Christ's crucifixion in Christian churches. Upon inquiring I was told that Japanese Christians are uncomfortable with this scene.

16. For Plotinus the reality of one human psyche in which all people participate is the basis of sharing feeling. Or did he derive his metaphysical explanation *from* his observation that, in fact, we are capable of sharing one another's experiences? *Ennead* 4.9.3

tertainment, but there is no mention in classical literature of compassion for the human beings who suffered and died in the coliseum. Similarly, in the *actae* describing Christian martyrdom, compassion for the martyr is seldom expressed. Christian martyrs were not considered victims, for in a sense they had *chosen* martyrdom. A few grains of incense thrown on the fire before the emperor's portrait would have sufficed to spare them.

Scarry asks, "How is it that one person can be in the presence of another person in pain and not know it—not know it to the point where he himself inflicts it, and goes on inflicting it?"[17] Compassion for others who suffer depends on the ability to imagine their suffering; "empathy (across class, sex, and national lines) depends on identification."[18] Historian Lynn Hunt argues that the popularity of epistolary novels in the eighteen century had a more than coincidental connection with the reform of punishment and execution at the same time in Britain and western Europe. The popularity of the eighteenth-century epistolary novel contributed strongly to the emerging public sensitivity to torture and execution. Novels about the poor enabled and encouraged the ruling class imaginatively to empathize with their sufferings: "Imagined empathy—not in the sense of made up, but in the sense that empathy requires a leap of faith, of imagining that someone else is like you."[19] Hunt writes,

> Reading accounts of torture . . . had physical effects that translated into brain changes and came

17. Scarry, *Body in Pain*, 12.
18. Hunt, *Inventing Human Rights*, 55.
19. Ibid., 32.

back out as new concepts about the organization of social and political life. New kinds of reading (and viewing and listening) created new individual experiences (empathy) which in turn made possible new social and political concepts (human rights).[20]

Samuel Richardson's *Pamela* (1740) and *Clarissa* (1747), Jean-Jacques Rousseau's *Julie* (1761), and many other epistolary novels were bestsellers. "Written by men, with women as protagonists, they became household names in the cities of western Europe, where [by the second half of the eighteenth century] literacy had increased 'to the point where even servants, male and female, read novels.'"[21] The contemporaneous appearance of the epistolary novel and the reform of punishment across Europe is striking.

> Judicial torture was abolished in Prussia in 1754; Sweden followed in 1772, Austria and Bohemia in 1776, France in the 1780s. In 1783 Great Britain introduced the mandatory use of "the drop" to reduce the suffering of the hanged. . . . In 1792 the guillotine was introduced in France. . . . As the American physician Benjamin Rush insisted in 1787, we should not forget that even criminals "possess souls and bodies composed of the same materials as those of our friends and relations. They are bone of our bone."[22]

Inability to imagine the suffering of others is a failure of *both* thought and feeling. Hannah Arendt's conclusion about the nature of Adolf Eichmann's crime (to be further

20. Ibid., 33–34.

21. Liew, *Reading Ideologies*, 162.

22. Hunt, *Inventing Human Rights*, 76.

discussed in chapter 6) was that he was unable to imagine the connection between what he did—making sure that trains to the extermination camps ran on schedule—and the murder of millions of Jews (and others).[23]

It is possible to alienate the rational mind and define the self by it, as Eichmann did.[24] The rational mind in isolation from the emotions cannot imagine the sufferings of others; that can only be done with the intelligent body, in which thinking and feeling are one activity. A major cost of thinking of "person" as a construction of separate and unevenly valued parts is that we are encouraged to view emotions as "unbridled irrationalism without any logic." The "logic of emotions" can be noticed—and valued—only when one thinks of "person" as an intelligent body in which rationality and emotion are simultaneous.[25]

Arne Vetlesen and others disagreed with Arendt's conclusion that Eichmann's crime was intellectual (the result of "thoughtlessness"): "The capacity Eichmann failed to exercise is emotional rather than intellectual or cognitive: it is the capacity to develop *empathy* with other human beings."[26] Indeed, the figure of Eichmann illustrates the ultimate distortion caused first by conceptualizing "person" as components, and second by identifying the

23. Hartouni, *Visualizing Atrocity*, 73.

24. "The evil [Arendt] encountered in the figure of Eichmann was better understood, she argued, as the outcome of a certain *thought-lessness* or inability to think from another's point of view. . . . 'He *merely . . . never realized what he was doing.'* It was sheer thoughtlessness—by no means identical with stupidity—that predisposed him to become one of the greatest criminals of that period" (Hartouni, *Visualizing Atrocity*, 17).

25. Stein, *Shameless*, 114.

26. Vetlesen, *Perception, Empathy, and Judgment*, 105.

self with one component of the person, whether rational mind or emotions. While the inadequacy of rational mind's activity, logic, is evident in Arendt's description of Eichmann's crime, emotions in isolation from thinking are an equally untrustworthy site for guidance in public affairs.[27] Ethical action requires the intelligent body's ability to think feelings and feel thoughts. Eichmann's inability to "think where he was not," that is, in another person's experience, together with his lack of empathy, define his failure: during his trial Eichmann said, "*Officially I had nothing to do with [the gassing] and, unofficially, I wasn't interested.*"[28]

At the outset of the Eichmann trial, in an effort to encourage objectivity, Chief Justice Robert Jackson "insisted that the documents be allowed to speak for themselves and that the prosecution construct its case *without* the emotionally compelling but evidentially compromised, because inevitably biased, testimony of those who had suffered under the boot of Nazi rule."[29] This effort at objectivity was undermined when, on the eighth day of the trial, the prosecution showed "emotionally compelling" images of the death camps. Images provoke feeling even more powerfully than language. In seeking objectivity, the trial—ineffectively—replicated Eichmann's crime, that is, the separation of rational mind from emotion. Clearly, it was impossible to ignore the suffering experienced by millions of people; the suffering was, indeed, the point of the trial.

27. "Emotions can be fickle, boundless, and easily co-opted in political life" (Hartouni, *Visualizing Atrocity*, 74).

28. Ibid., 81.

29. Quoted by Hartouni, *Visualizing Atrocity*, 97.

Academics are acutely uncomfortable when confronted with the emotional engagement of an author—Advocacy scholarship is when an author acknowledges and advocates an "interested" perspective, and Holocaust scholarship is perhaps the best-known example of scholarship that does not pretend objectivity, but seeks openly to persuade the reader to a certain perspective.

Sharing Suffering

Hospice volunteering is one way to participate in the suffering of another human being. I trained as a hospice volunteer in 2005. The training took six weeks and was largely committed to reassuring a group of scared but determined people that we *could*, yes, actually *could* do this work. Trainees had myriad questions about hypothetical situations, questions that were usually answered with "just be yourself" or "trust your instincts." These answers seemed to me at best frustratingly vague, at worst clichés. I recall thinking on hearing this advice that my instincts might be trustworthy about 20 percent of the time, but what about the other 80 percent?

We were instructed in hospice do's and don'ts. The "hospice handhold" is an example: The volunteer was to place her hand *under* the patient's hand so that if at any time the patient didn't want to hold hands, he could easily remove it. Also, we were, of course, to feel compassion for our patient but should not become personal friends with her or her family, maintaining at all times a slight but respectful professional distance. When the patient's death was imminent and family members arrived, the volunteer was to back off, sit in another room, unless specifically invited to be at the bedside. When the patient died, "tears may run down your face," we were told, "but you must not sob." Sobbing would indicate that our own sorrows were erupting into the situation. I understood these injunctions only later, when circumstances made them relevant.

Sheila, my second hospice patient, was ninety years old when I met her. She suffered from congestive heart failure. She lived for over three years. Obedient to the state ruling that hospice care must not exceed six months, Sheila "graduated" several times, returning to hospice when she took a turn for the worse. Once she said to me, "I don't know what's wrong with me. I can't seem to die on schedule."

Sheila told me that when she was six or seven, she was frequently accused of "killing Jesus" by other children on the playground. "But Sheila," I said, "Jews didn't kill Jesus; Romans did." She stared at me in astonishment. "Why didn't I know that eighty-five years ago?" she said.

"It's important to be strong," she told me. "I am a strong woman, even now." When I left her at the end of an afternoon, she always said, "Be strong." I assured her that I would. She told me that she had learned as a young woman that it's not that you simply are—or aren't—strong. In many situations, strength is a *choice*. She told me how she learned this: When she was a young woman, her father was killed by a thief in his small shop in Chicago. She was in the shop when the gunman entered; her father was in a back room doing paperwork. He heard strange sounds and came into the shop to investigate. Seeing a gun pressed into his daughter's back he rushed at the man and was shot repeatedly. When her father was killed, her mother and brother "went to pieces," Sheila said. She knew that someone would have to run the business, and she determined to do so. "I would have loved to fall apart," Sheila said, "but I didn't have time. I had to be strong." Hospice volunteering involved not only sharing another's suffering. It was also hugely rewarding. Compassion grows in sitting with a suffering person, simply listening.

Music was a large part of Sheila's childhood. When Russian Jewish friends visited the family's Chicago home, there was always music. A cousin played jazz violin; someone else played piano; there was singing and dancing. There was wonderful food, too—heavy on the onions and garlic. Sheila liked to listen to her CD of Russian gypsy music; often a tear or two ran down her face as she listened. One afternoon, as we were listening, I heard a small sound that I realized wasn't on the CD. It was Sheila, singing in a little girl's small voice. There was a picture of Sheila at the age of seven beside her bed. The little girl, with a slightly quizzical expression, had been dressed to look like a child movie star whom people said she resembled. I looked at that picture as Sheila was singing in her thin voice; I knew that I was hearing the voice of that small girl.

Suffering and compassion, the topics discussed in this chapter, may seem to be simply feelings, but feeling and thinking are not separable for the intelligent body. The intelligent body produces thought deeply informed by feeling and feeling that is thoughtful. Thought and feeling are not delegated to different parts of the person. Chapter 6 will consider further how "thinking" might differ when we imagine it as proceeding no longer from the rational mind in isolation but from an intelligent body.

6

Intelligent Bodies Think

We beg you, make us truly alive.
—SERAPION OF THMUIS, FOURTH CENTURY

To think and to be fully alive are the same.
—HANNAH ARENDT[1]

What makes my *Thinker* think is that he thinks
not only with his brain, his knitted brow, his
distended nostrils and compressed lips, but with
every muscle of his arms, back, and legs, with his
clenched fist and gripping toes.
—AUGUSTE RODIN

In Part One, "From Stacked Components to the Intelligent Body," I discussed the gradual isolation of thinking from feeling and the location of these activities in different components of a person. After Descartes'

1. Arendt, *Thinking*, 178.

cogito ergo sum, broad consensus that a person is an assemblage of parts became a "silent thought," an unquestioned assumption. Reuniting the activities of thinking and feeling entails a blurring of (by now) firmly established boundaries that insist that rational thought is done in something called mind, while feeling occurs in something called body.

Thinking/feeling is an activity of an intelligent body. In the preceding chapter I have imagined how we might *feel* differently if feeling were not isolated from thinking. In this chapter I endeavor to imagine thinking/feeling as one activity of an intelligent body. Language doesn't help this enterprise; as Plato observed, the only language we have is that of analysis and description, different names describing a single activity. Stuck, as were our forebears, with the only language we have, I *differentiate* thinking/feeling only for purposes of focus and description. We will need to backtrack a bit in order to propose a countercultural approach to the activity of thinking/feeling.

The Evolution of Thinking

Why have professional "thinkers"—especially philosophers and theologians—been so insistent on separating thinking and feeling? I have made several attempts to answer this question, which seems to be quite complex; here I suggest that a need to distinguish humans from the so-called lower animals has been at least part of the motivation. Maxine Sheets-Johnstone's essay "Taking Evolution Seriously: A Matter of Primate Intelligence" considers persistent efforts to support the claim that, due to some presumed attribute, humans are different *in kind* from other animals. She examines the arguments for human uniqueness—intelligence, language, tool-using, tool-making, etc.—and concludes that none of these is unique to humans; rather, they are simply "philosophical justifications for cherishing ourselves," in short, human arrogance.[2] Joel Green proposes another mark of distinction for humans, namely, that we are made in the "image of God."[3] A long tradition supports this claim, but it is not discussed by evolutionary biologists.

Sheets-Johnstone argues that there are no breaks in evolution; all species, including humans, *evolved*. This means that capacities found in so-called lower animals are continuous with human capacities, though differently developed.

> Human rationality and human language are themselves products of evolution, and not in the sense of novel neural brain circuitry gradually (much less suddenly) appearing such that communally understood words began sprouting from the mouths of a few no-doubt-surprised-because-heretofore-verbally-mute hominids, but in the sense of actual living creatures *inventing* new modes of behavior.[4]

In fact, she writes, great apes are better than humans at some activities, such as brachiating, that is, swinging from tree limb to tree limb across a forest!

2. Sheets-Johnstone, *Corporeal Turn*, 125.
3. Green, *Body, Soul, and Human Life*, 61–62.
4. Sheets-Johnstone, *Corporeal Turn*, 121–22.

What Is Thinking?

> Thinking in its non-cognitive, non-specialized
> sense . . . is not a prerogative of the few but an
> ever-present faculty in everybody; the inability
> to think is not a failure of the many who lack
> brain power but an ever-present possibility for
> everybody—scientists, scholars, and other spe-
> cialists in mental enterprises not excluded.[5]

The kind of rationality that a society recognizes and
trains is *historical*, intimately related to the circumstances
with which it attempts to deal. To think with the intelligent body is not only to analyze the development of
ideas and their relationship to one another, but to consider the *circumstances*, the conversations, institutions,
and loyalties (both social and intellectual) within which
the author speaks. I gave as an example Socrates' proof of
the immortality of the soul, spoken (according to Plato)
minutes before Socrates' death, and thus hardly a disinterested "proof."

By the standard of the component model of person,
so little of what we call "thinking" really *is* thinking; we
use the word to cover a very wide range of mental operations. Thinking is partly traversing well-worn and
predictable brain paths; it consists partly of impressions
that have stuck, partly of settled biases, partly of partial,
unexamined, selected facts, together with the feeling of
the moment. Although rational thought (on the components model) explicitly disallows feeling, feeling is never
absent; it can only be ignored. Intellectual and emotional
loyalties and one's perspective are always included, even

5. Arendt, *Thinking*, 191.

if concealed and unacknowledged. What would it be like to *feel* a thought? We know what sexual thoughts feel like, but at what level of abstraction do thoughts lose their feeling tone?

Aristotle's "law of excluded middle," discussed in his treatise *On Interpretation,* is one of the foundations of logic. It states that "for any proposition, either that proposition is true or its contradiction is." And "it is impossible that there should be anything between the two parts of a contradiction." Logic's limitations are immediately evident, for in life, almost *everything* is in the middle. In fact, Aristotle recognized this and attempted to warn against misapplication of the axiom. His first formulation of the axiom of non-contradiction stated explicitly that this law applies "to the discourse *within the soul.*" In other words, the axiom of non-contradiction has important limitations; it should not be applied to life. Arendt comments, "We can watch how such an insight, won from the factual experience of the thinking ego, gets lost when it is generalized into a philosophical doctrine."[6]

Let it be acknowledged that there were also some distinct advantages in separating rational thought from feelings and emotions. Rationality is a historically situated skill, exceedingly important and valuable in the context in which it received its greatest development. Rationality came to be highly valued in the midst of the religious emotionality of the Hundred Years' War (1337–1453) and the Wars of Religion (1524–1648). People hoped fervently that rational thought would halt religious frenzy. Designed specifically within and for these circumstances,

6. Ibid., 186.

does it still serve us well? Michel Foucault's warning, "Everything is dangerous," applies to rationality.[7]

Consider a twentieth-century description of the danger of isolating thinking from feeling. Hannah Arendt's analysis of Adolf Eichmann's trial strongly suggests that the thinking required in modern Western societies must include feeling. Because Eichmann excluded feeling, he was unable to imagine the effects on others of his participation in the "giant machinery of Nazism."[8] Arendt named Eichmann's crime "thoughtlessness," defining thoughtlessness as the "inability to think from another's point of view."[9] The opposite of thoughtlessness is empathy, the "ability to think from where one is not."[10] Thoughtlessness is an incapacity with moral significance and effects.

However, the practice of empathy is not simply allowing feeling to flood and distort thinking. It is, rather, a specific kind of thinking, one for which knowing oneself is essential. Thinking/feeling is "a practice of self-examination and accountability," not, primarily, "for the purpose of establishing affective ties with other individuals or knowing where they stand or what they might feel but as a way of determining and evaluating (by contrast) where one stands oneself. . . . [It is] an encounter of the

7. "My point is not that everything is bad, but that everything is dangerous, which is not exactly the same as bad. If everything is dangerous, then we always have something to do" (Foucault, "On the Genealogy of Ethics," in Dreyfus and Rabinow, *Michel Foucault*, 231–32).

8. Quoted by Hartouni, *Visualizing Atrocity*, 84.

9. Ibid., 17.

10. Ibid., 74.

self with itself."[11] Arendt observes, "When Socrates goes home he is not alone, he is by himself."[12]

In a "'thinking dialogue" with myself, "I dismantle and re-narrativize my life and history and the assumptions and convictions that structure both."[13] Only after understanding myself am I free to empathize with others. Adolf Eichmann's "rationality" demonstrates that rationality, isolated from feeling, can be overdeveloped, producing and supporting the atrocities of the modern world.

Developing "Thoughtfulness": Reading

Rational minds, in isolation from feeling, are always in danger of what Arendt called thoughtlessness. But it is insufficient to simply say that one *should* be thoughtful. How can thoughtfulness—the ability to know oneself and empathize with another—be developed intentionally? In *Inventing Human Rights,* historian Lynn Hunt argues that public sensitivity to the suffering of others coincided with the origin and popularity of the epistolary novel in eighteenth-century England: "There is remarkable chronological coincidence between the emergence of epistolary novels, the reform of punishment, and the birth of human rights."[14]

The latter eighteenth century saw the reform of punishment and execution across Europe and in the United

11. Ibid., 74–76.

12. Arendt, *Thinking*, 187.

13. Quoted by Hartouni, *Visualizing Atrocity*, 76.

14. Hunt, *Inventing Human Rights*, 163.

States. Hunt suggests that epistolary novels detailing the suffering of poor women (written by men) actually changed the sensibilities of the public, encouraging reform of public torture and execution. For example, the regular use of "the drop" was introduced to reduce the suffering of the executed (hanged). Hasty executions also minimized the chance that crowds, which now found the sight of a hanged criminal twisting in anguish at the end of a rope morally repellent, might overpower the executioner and stop the execution.[15]

Given access to the inner lives of characters as well as to descriptions of their physical sufferings, readers began to develop not only intersubjectivity—a heightened sense of identification with the emotions and thoughts of another person—but also intercorporeality—the ability to imagine others' physical experience as one's own.[16]

The twentieth-century philosopher Susanne Langer wrote,

> There is . . . an important part of reality that is quite inaccessible to the formative influence of language: that is the realm of so-called inner experience, the life of feeling and emotion. The reason why language is so powerless here is not, as many people suppose, that feeling and emotion are irrational; on the contrary, they seem irrational because language does not help to make them conceivable and most people cannot conceive anything without the logical scaffolding of words.[17]

15. Foucault, *Discipline and Punish*, 64.
16. Liew, *Reading Ideologies*, 162.
17. Langer, *Philosophical Sketches*, 79.

Feeling is authorized and its expression is trained by the books we read, the music we listen to, and the images we live with, by the art forms of daily life. "The primary function of art is to objectify feeling so that we can contemplate and understand it."[18]

Thinking Together

> What's said is often less important than the tone of voice in which the words are spoken. There is music in dialogue, mysterious harmonies and dissonances that vibrate in the body like a tuning fork.[19]

Dialogue is another method for increasing thoughtfulness. Conversation with a person who is able and willing to speak both honestly and deeply can challenge and expand one's knowledge, both of oneself and of the other.[20] My example is Augustine's distinction between ordinary conversation and dialogue.

Augustine learned—however indirectly—what talking together, *facie ad faciem,* can achieve from Plato's description of dialectic.[21] Plato characterized dialectic as the method for understanding "the very essence of each thing."[22] There is, Plato said, no other way "to determine

18. Ibid., chap. 1, fn. 8.
19. Hustveldt, *Sorrows of an American*, 293.
20. Bussanich, "Plotinus's Metaphysics of the One," 41.
21. *Republic* VII. 532a.
22. Ibid., 532b.

what each thing really is."[23] "Is not dialectic the only process of inquiry that advances in this manner, doing away with hypotheses ... Dialectic gently draws [the eye of the soul] forth and leads it up."[24]

Augustine's favorite Scripture verse, quoted more frequently than any other throughout his career, was 1 Corinthians 13:12: "*Videmus nunc per speculum in aenigmate; tunc autem facie ad faciem*" ("We see now through a glass darkly; then, however, face to face"). In his *Confessions* he described several occasions on which he received a foretaste of *facie ad faciem* by talking with someone. Augustine described this process in *Confessions* 9.10. He and his mother, Monica, were

> alone and talking together and very sweet our talk was. . . . We were discussing between ourselves . . . what the eternal life of the saints could be like; . . . with our affections burning still more strongly we raised ourselves higher. . . . And still we went upward, meditating and speaking and looking with wonder at your works. . . . And as we talked, yearning toward this Wisdom, we did, with the whole strength of our hearts' impulse, just lightly come into touch with her, and we sighed . . . and we returned to the sounds made by our mouths.

Dialectic requires that the conversation partners have similar *enough* perspectives that they hold some fundamental common assumptions, but *different* enough that each person's perspective is challenged, corrected, and refined by the other's.

23. Ibid., 533b.
24. Ibid., 533d.

Intelligent Bodies Think

Do intelligent bodies *think* better than rational minds? Intelligent bodies' thinking works with more, and more varied, information than do rational minds. In her book *The Powers of Horror*, French psychoanalyst Julia Kristeva argues that abjection, the horrific—"what disturbs identity, system, order"—is the basis of "religious, moral, and ideological codes."[25] Civilization, she says, requires that abjection—refuse and corpses—be concealed, denied, rendered invisible, and "permanently thrust aside in order to live."[26] Kristeva assumes the components model of human persons, identifying one important function of rationality as hiding the reality of physical life. I propose, rather, that the messiness of physical life is insistently recognized and represented within Christianity. Images of the abject crucified Christ, the nursing virgin who has recently given messy human birth to her son, accounts of the torture and martyrdom of saints—all describe and make visible birth, death, blood, and suffering. Far from being predominantly spiritual, the history of Christianity is often embarrassingly replete with bodies, gore, and horror. Intelligent bodies cannot eliminate abjection from thinking.

The rational mind in isolation is willing to sacrifice sensitivity and nuance for clarity. However, body, isolated from rational mind, often sacrifices clarity for life's necessary *mixtus*. While rational mind has *knowledge* that is inevitably perspectival and limited, body has *experience* that is equally problematic. Experience may be more

25. Kristeva, *Powers of Horror*, 209.
26. Ibid., 3.

emotionally vivid than knowledge, but it has limited pre-diction value. As we go through life collecting experience, it becomes difficult to experience new circumstances *freshly.* The "double ignorance" becomes a limitation. Because we have *seen* what happened in a somewhat similar situation in the past, we do not know that we do not know what will occur in this *new* situation. In short, we stop *seeing freshly*; we stop *learning* from new experience.

Imposing former experience on new circumstances indicates that we are motivated by fear. The experiences we tend to remember were usually painful or difficult; in fact, our culture calls painful experiences "learning experiences." Why don't we learn from joyful experiences? Perhaps we regard the pleasure of the experience as an end in itself, so we do not think about what we can learn from it. It requires no hidden salvific value as does painful learning experience.

Augustine and the Intelligent Body

Augustine described the problem created by the classical definition of "person" as composed of hierarchically arranged soul and body. At first he could not conceptualize God as anything but body—hugely extended body, but still, body. Influenced by Stoic teaching that only a body was capable of moving another body, he "considered that whatever was not extended in space, whether diffused or condensed or swelling out or having some such qualities or being capable of having them, must be, in the full sense of the word, nothing."[27]

27. *Confessions* 7.1.

Subsequently he learned from books by Platonists "to look for a truth that is incorporeal."[28] But he did not find in these books "that the Word was made flesh and dwelt among men."[29] He did not find a new valuing of body. "I was afraid to believe that He was born in the flesh lest I should be forced to believe that He was defiled by the flesh."[30] Augustine was not, he said, as yet humble enough to recognize the important lesson to be learned from Jesus' humanity. The incarnation revealed "divinity in the weakness that it had put on by wearing our 'coat of skin.'"[31]

Augustine's life project, carrying over psychic "weight" from fear to love,[32] included a reevaluation of body. As we have seen, Arendt labeled Eichmann's inability to empathize with the Nazis' victims "thoughtlessness." Thoughtfulness, empathy, is *thinking with the intelligent body*, the ability and willingness to stand in the shoes of another person, imagining her pain. Fear disables this ability.

Augustine watched his body to learn what he felt/ thought. At the moment of conversion, he said, "my face changed" (*mutato vultu*; 8.12).[33] How did he know? Was

28. Ibid., 7.20.

29. Ibid., 7.9.

30. Ibid., 5.10.

31. Ibid., 7.18.

32. Augustine, *Confessions* 13.9: "My weight is my love; by it I am carried wherever I am carried."

33. The Latin *mutato vultu* might be translated more precisely as "my expression changed." *Vultu* designates expression, while *facie* refers to facial features. *Facie ad faciem*, Augustine's phrase for perfect knowledge, refers to *seeing* the other *in the flesh,* in the actual facial features.

he looking in a mirror? No! He *felt* his conversion *in his face*. And what did he feel? He gave a clue in *Confessions* 7.14; as he began to narrate his conversion, he wrote, "I relaxed a little from myself" (*cessavi de me paululum*). He felt the myriad tiny muscles in his face let go, relax. A minute later, he says, "By now my face was perfectly calm" (*tranquillo iam vultu*).

Augustine's face was an especially sensitive barometer of his thoughts and emotions. From the infant who "turned pale and looked bitterly at another infant sharing his milk"—for Augustine a confirmation of original sin—to *facie ad faciem*, his description of ideal vision, Augustine's face revealed his most private thoughts and feelings.

7

Intelligent Bodies Believe

"To carry out the mystery of unity we ourselves
receive from him the body that he himself
received from us."

—Fourth Lateran Council, 1st canon

"To confess the faith, love suffices."

—Jean-Luc Marion[1]

A cover article in the *New York Times Book Review*[2] claims that exploration of Christian belief in the lives of fictional characters has disappeared from contemporary novels. Novelists avoid individuals' religious struggles, according to the author, Paul Elie. Although "Christianity is highly visible in public life . . . [it is] marginal or of no consequence in a great many individual lives." Marilynne Robinson's *Gilead* may appear to be an exception. In her deeply religious character, the Reverend

1. Marion, *God Without Being*, 195.
2. Elie, "Has Fiction Lost Its Faith?"

John Ames, "belief is believable," Elie writes, because it is "so plainly the fruit of a personal search." Yet Robinson's novel is "set in the past, concerned with a clergyman, [and] presents belief as a family matter, animated by a social crisis."[3]

> Belief as upbringing, belief as social fact, belief as a species of American weirdness: our literary fiction has all of these things. All that is missing is the believer. . . . Belief hasn't been understood [Elie concludes] until the serious writers have had their say.[4]

I suggest that the problem of making belief believable to contemporary readers is caused by an almost unquestioned but false understanding of what it means to believe. There is general consensus that belief occurs when the rational mind accepts a litany of creedal assertions. Underlying that misconception of what belief *is,* is a conceptualization of the human person as a collection of distinguishable, even separable, components controlled (at best) by a dictator, rational mind. Perhaps the struggle to believe is not attractive material for contemporary novelists because it is assumed that this would entail a dry narration of ideas.

This idea of belief has caused untold numbers of people to find belief impossible and to feel scorn for believers. A huge contemporary literature attacks religious belief of every kind. The "prideful rational mind"[5] cannot give credence to accounts of a human God or a doctrine

3. Ibid., 14.
4. Ibid, 15.
5. Loy, *Lack and Transcendence*, 26–27.

such as the resurrection of body. Valuing honesty and scientific principles, the rational mind sacrifices religious beliefs that could be life-orienting and enhancing. The pain of this sacrifice is manifest in American society as well as in individual lives. Why do we so unquestioningly trust the poorly and partially informed rational mind? Is there another way to believe besides the rational mind's assent to doctrines?

The *Confessions,* Augustine's description of the operation of grace in his life, is a novel—in the sense that all autobiographies have a fictional component—that has been fascinating to generations of readers. How does grace operate in a human life? We might think of the alternatives, as Hindus do, as the cat-carrying method or the monkey-carrying method. The cat-carrying method can be summarized in the words of Martin Luther's mantra, given to him by his confessor and friend, Johan von Staupitz: "I am yours; save me" (*Tuus sum ego; salvum me fac*; Ps 119:94). In the cat-carrying method, the kitten goes utterly limp; the mother cat picks it up by the neck with her teeth and carries the kitten, dangling helplessly. In the monkey-carrying method, on the other hand, the baby monkey leaps onto its mother's back and hangs on for dear life as its mother leaps from tree limb to tree limb.

Augustine's strenuous pursuit of mental and physical resolution seems to resemble the monkey-carrying method. He used the metaphor of the visual ray to suggest that both viewer and object have a role to play. This theory of vision assumes a quasi-physical ray, lit by the fire that warms and animates the body, at its most intense in the eye. The ray unites viewer and object as it projects from the eye to *touch* its object. The visual ray is a two-way street; the object then moves back up the visual ray to imprint itself on the brain. Augustine contrasts vision with hearing in order to emphasize that vision is not, like hearing, passive; any sound of a certain loudness in one's vicinity is heard. The viewer, on the other hand, must cleanse, strengthen, train, and focus the eye on its object. Augustine described this process in detail in his treatise on the Trinity.

Yet Augustine also insisted on his own passivity in relation to God's action. Here his image might be described as the cat-carrying method. He described God's action in his life as *fovisti caput*; God turned his head, the image is tactile.

> You [God] soothed my head, unknown to me,
> and closed my eyes lest they see vanity; I relaxed
> a little from myself, and my madness was lulled
> to sleep. I awoke in you . . .[6]

Augustine says (metaphorically) that he was converted *in his sleep*. What stronger image of passivity could there be? Yet his intense struggle and activity (on the one hand) and his passivity in God's hands (on the other) must somehow be balanced in the reader's mind. Augustine experienced both. His use of conflicting metaphors to describe his struggle mirrors that struggle. Was God the only actor in Augustine's life, or was his own anguished struggle an essential part of the resolution? Conflicting images of struggle and relaxation can both be true, not reducible to one or the other. Intelligent bodies can *live* feelings and images that appear contradictory to rational minds.

6. *Confessions* 7.14.

And, as previously mentioned, it was Augustine's intelligent body that experienced conversion. Augustine *felt* belief as a relaxation of body.

Doctrine and the Intelligent Body: Original Sin

Not only would we understand the liturgical and devotional *practices* of Christianity as central and essential if we change our "silent thought" about what belief is, we might also understand Christian doctrines differently. Consider, for example, the doctrine of original sin. G. K. Chesterton once said that original sin is the *only* Christian doctrine that is fully documented; any newspaper, on any day, will give ample testimony to the perversity of human nature.

Augustine is the earliest Christian theologian who found the origin of sin in human bodies. He thought he saw original sin in infant behavior. At first, he said, the infant is nothing but "life and a body."[7] *Instinctively* she sucks nourishment from a woman's breast (nourishment that is generously provided, Augustine specifies, not by the nurse herself, but by God). But the infant's first *intentional* (as opposed to *instinctual*) act, he said, is sinful. He asked, "Who can recall to me the sin I did in my infancy?" Unable to observe his own infancy, he extrapolates from his observation of another baby (perhaps his son, Adeodatus; he doesn't say). The baby he observed "was envious; it could not yet speak but it turned pale and looked bitterly at another baby sharing its milk." He declared that infants are harmless because of physical weak-

7. Ibid., 1.7.

ness, "not because of innocence."[8] The inability of infants to speak insures that they are helpless victims of adults' interpretations and projections!

Augustine thought of infant behavior as aggressively sinful, extending the neonate's instinctive gasp/grasp for breath to the greedy behavior of the adult, grasping at everything that crosses his path in the fear that something will be missed. Augustine described the continuity of this grasping in detail:

> For it is just these same sins which, as the years pass by, become related no longer to tutors, schoolmasters, footballs, nuts, and pet sparrows, but to magistrates and kings, gold, estates, and slaves . . .[9]

A clarification is necessary. The doctrine of original sin is not *based* on Augustine's claim that infants' first intentional act is sinful, but on St. Paul's statement that all humans share Adam's sin. Before Augustine, Tertullian interpreted Paul as describing the existence of a *vitium originalis* (original weakness). Augustine took the next step, articulating a *peccatum originalis* (original sin). He specified that *peccatum originalis* includes not only the *possibility* of sin, but also its actuality, or "original guilt"; all humans, simply by being born, he said, share the guilt of Adam's sin.

Augustine also volunteered the innovation that original sin is inherited through sex; the transmission of original sin occurs, he said, at the moment of conception. This claim was *confirmed* for him by the allegedly "jeal-

8. Ibid.
9. Ibid., 1. 19.

ous"—the already sinful—infant. Individuals reiterate the experience of the species; ontogeny recapitulates phylogeny. Moreover, Augustine's often repeated principle that any good in the individual is to be attributed directly to God makes it evident that the infant's first *intentional* (rather than instinctual) act must necessarily be sinful.

Sin, damage to oneself and others, may be too well documented to be arguable, but is it the whole story? Thanks to Paul and Augustine it is certainly the feature of human existence that Christianity has *noticed,* analyzed, and addressed. But, I ask again, is it the whole story?

Still observing the allegedly jealous infant, Augustine remarked that as an infant he must have smiled "first when I was asleep, and later when I was awake,"[10] implying that the infant's smile is extrapolated from the sleeping grimace. Had he lingered to explore the infant's first smile (at approximately two to three months of age) and its implications, he might have found it necessary to revise his teaching that the infant's first *intentional* act—what is "original" to the infant and to the human race—is sin.

From extensive contemporary studies, psychiatrist René Spitz concludes that the infant's smile is significant. It is, he says, "the first sign of recognition of another that, in its gesture of amiability, carries with it a moral tone: [namely], to be open and friendly toward others. . . . [It is] a spontaneous, individual, affectively charged, kinetic act."[11] And the infant's smile does not, as we might think, merely imitate the mother's smiling face. It is an *intentional*, initiatory act, demonstrated by the fact that blind babies smile.

10. Ibid., 1.6.

11. Quoted by Sheets-Johnstone, *Roots of Morality,* 352.

Babies' intentional smile occurs at about two to three months; fear reactions to environmental circumstances, such as sudden loud noises or loss of support, occur at about the same time. These are instinctive reactions, however, not reactions to other human beings. The first antisocial respone occurs as "stranger anxiety" at approximately nine months, much later than the first smile. Studies of infants suggest, then, that we should speak, not of "original sin," but of original amiability or friendliness.

If twenty-first-century secular people can be helped to find the comfort and challenge of Christian beliefs, it will not be by rational explanation of a mind-boggling doctrine such as the resurrection of body. It can only be by changing the meaning of belief and the understanding of the human person. In an age of secularism based on belief in science, the honest rational mind cannot believe in the resurrection of body. But perhaps an intelligent body can believe the doctrine. I explore this possibility next.

Resurrection of Body

We long not to die. Belief in the resurrection of body acknowledges this longing and allows it to inform *present* life, weaves it into devotional and liturgical practice, into everyday life.

Augustine said in a sermon,

> I know you want to keep on living. You do not want to die. And you want to pass from this life to another in such a way that you will not rise again as a dead person, but fully alive and

transformed. This is what you desire; *this is the deepest human feeling.*[12]

Augustine acknowledged longing for resurrection of body. Many centuries later, Woody Allen also longs for an embodied immortality: "I don't want to be immortal through my work; I want to be immortal by *not dying*. And I don't want to live on in the hearts and minds of my countrymen; I want to live on in my apartment."[13] Where does this longing come from? Maxine Sheets-Johnstone argues that the longing for immortality arises from greed that constantly demands *more*: "more power, more status, more privilege. The mere fact of being alive carries with it the desire for *more*. It is thus not surprising that the meaning of one's life readily becomes attached to *more* in the form of a meaning that endures beyond one's lifetime."[14]

In short, "immortality ideologies," she writes, are the result of rational mind's "greedy desire for *more*." If, however, we examine the intelligent body's "*deepest human feeling*," we must begin with the infant's instinctive gasp/grasp for breath, for life. This is, as Augustine wrote, "the deepest human feeling," based not on rational mind's greed but on intelligent body's longing for *more life*. In the face of the deepest human feeling, the rational mind must remain agnostic, clinging neither to an "immortality ideology" nor to stubborn denial of the bodily resurrection.

Plato's "double ignorance" lies at the root of *both* immortality ideologies *and* the insistence that death is final.

---

12. Augustine, *Sermon* 344.4. My italics.

13. *Love and Death*, written and directed by Woody Allen (United Artists, 1975).

14. Sheets-Johnstone, *Roots of Morality*, 158.

We do not *know. And we do not know that we do not know.*
Those of us who believe and those of us who deny have
convinced ourselves that we know: the double ignorance.
And the more we don't know, the more loudly and insistently we proclaim that we *know.* Yet we call it "belief" in
the resurrection of body precisely because we don't know.
The strong claim that we *know* does reveal the greed of
the rational mind, artificially isolated from body.

Longing for the resurrection of body is different
from longing for the immortality of soul or rational
mind. An immortality ideology proposes to identify the
person with soul/mind, sacrificing the biodegradable
body. Longing for immortality *is* rational mind's greed
for more. It imagines the self-perpetuation of soul/mind
only, not of body. But intelligent bodies believe differently than do rational minds. The intelligent body does
not require rational mind's assent. Neither does it insist
on understanding how resurrection of body *works*, as
science would seek to understand. On the doctrine of
the resurrection of body, rational mind must accept the
discipline of agnosticism: we don't know, and we know that
we don't know.

Inability to believe in the resurrection of body is
intimately connected to the disparaged body of the components model of person. Augustine, inheritor of the
classical analysis of person as "something called soul" and
"something called body," had the same problem. He "con-
fesses" that as a youth he "had not the slightest notion of
the mystery contained in 'The Word was made flesh.'"[15]
He simply could not understand that in the person of

15. *Confessions* 7.19.

Jesus, God would not be contaminated by appearing in our "coats of skin."

The Intelligent Body's Belief

As stated above, if we examine the "deepest human feeling," we must begin with the infant's gasp/grasp of breath. If we think of the infant as an intelligent body that knows when to roll over, when to sit up, when to walk, we notice that the infant's instinct is to grasp *more life*. This is where the longing for *more life* originates. From the perspective of the infant person as intelligent body, however, the infant's first, most primitive instinct is to want *more life*; the adult's "deepest human feeling" is continuous with the infant's grasp of breath. Belief in the resurrection of body begins with the infant's gasp/grasp of *life*.

Intelligent bodies believe differently than do rational minds. Although Augustine was constrained by an assumption, a "silent thought" that insisted that the human person consisted of soul and body, he implicitly used another model. He proposed that the Christian's belief consists of longing, that is, of *living out into* that for which it longs. If belief in resurrection of body is, most fundamentally, present longing, the resurrection of body is *now;* it is how one lives today. "The whole life of the Christian is a holy longing. What you long for, as yet you do not see. . . . That is our life, to be exercised by longing."[16]

Augustine used the practice of fasting to demonstrate how longing acts in the intelligent body. *Desiderium sinus cordis* ("longing makes the heart deep"), Augustine

16. Augustine, *Tractatus in epistolam Joannis ad Parthos* 4.6.

wrote in his treatise on fasting, *De utilitate jejunii* (*The Usefulness of Fasting*). "When they are hungry, they stretch out; while they are stretching, they are enlarged; while they are enlarged, they become capacious, and, when they have become capacious enough, they will be filled in due time."[17] A change in the intelligent body's practice is a change in the person. It is not, as usually interpreted, that body's experience is transferable to mind, but that the intelligent body reacts directly.

Lest anyone think of longing as passive, Augustine hastily assures his readers that longing is composed of desire, delight, and love—activity, not passivity: *inardescimus et imus* ("we are inflamed and we go").[18] Augustine's congregation shouted out in acclamation and applauded when he described love's activity:

> Love has feet, which take us to the Church, love
> has hands which give to the poor, love has eyes
> which give knowledge of him who is in need. . . .
> Love has ears. . . . He that has love sees the whole
> at once with the understanding's grasp.[19]

Love is not a state into which one "falls" passively, as usually represented in American media. It is something individuals and societies actively *make*. Augustine exhorts his congregation to *make* love.

Pilgrimage is the metaphor Augustine used to describe the life of longing. He described a long process of *becoming* Christian, shifting the immense glacial weight of the psyche from fear to love: *pondeus meum amore*

17. *De utilitate jejunii* 1.

18. *Confessions* 13.9

19. Augustine, *Homilies on I John* VII.10.

meus; eo feror quacumque feror ("My weight is my love; by it I am carried wherever I am carried")—a daily pilgrimage.[20] *This* is the "conversion" his *Confessions* describes, the gradual movement of his intelligent body to belief, *simultaneously mental and physical.* This was not his famous dramatic conversion as described in Book 8, which was only a moment in the incremental conversion he described in the *Confessions,* a movement both occurring *before* and continuing long *after* the moment in the garden.[21]

We must ask, I think, not only what doctrines *mean,* but also what they *do.* Doctrines are performative; they act on the believer. So then, what does the doctrine of resurrection of the body *do,* and why do we need it? Does it simply extend mind's greed for *more* to infinity? Is it important to believe in the resurrection of body if one seeks to *become* Christian? I think it is, not only because multiple scriptural and liturgical sources say that it is, but because this belief directly affects how I live *now,* how I think of myself and other human beings, how in my large and small daily habits I relate to the earth's body and the whole whirling universe. This doctrine is one of the very few suggestions I can find in the provisions of my culture that helps me think of bodies as anything other than briefly pleasurable (or painful) and ultimately biodegradable.

What might be some of the real effects of believing in the resurrection of body with my intelligent body? When we begin with the infant's intelligent body that knows

20. Augustine, *Confessions* 13.9.

21. Book 10 of the *Confessions* discusses the many "conversions" still to be negotiated—from wet dreams to enticing smells—long after the Book 8 "conversion."

when to roll over, when to sit up, when to walk, we notice that the infant's first, most primitive instinct—that first gasp/grasp of breath—is to want *more life*. Extrapolated from the infant's intelligent body is the adult's "deepest human feeling," namely, the desire for *more life*.

We (as a society) do not love and care for our bodies. Our habits of acquisitiveness and hedonism are *hard* on bodies. The body that media culture wants for us is the "I want it all now" body, a body that consumes continuously but remains slender, athletic, and energetic (I could add white and young). Media images have what Michel Foucault called "strong power," namely, the power of attraction. As long as strong power is working, he said, there is no need for "weak power," that is, coercion. In our culture, bodies are not site and symbol of subjectivity, but are commodified and made spectacle. We desperately need the doctrine of the resurrection of body because it effectively revalues body, not only our own bodies, but it prompts us to notice the suffering of others and of the earth's abused body.

The seventeenth-century Anglican priest Thomas Traherne observed that "what we misapprehend we cannot use."[22] Because we have thought of the doctrine of the resurrection of body as something to be believed by the rational mind, we have not seen its relevance to living Christian lives, that is, to "making love" now, in our society, in the present.

Christianity has traditionally been very concerned about the dangers of attachment to power and possessions, but the equal dangers of passivity, cynicism, and

22. Traherne, *Centuries of Meditations*, 4.16.

indifference to the suffering and struggling of other living beings have not been articulated as frequently or as forcefully. The religious and intellectual traditions of the West have neglected the urgencies of this world in favor of attention to another world.

Similarly, until the second half of the twentieth century it was not possible to identify and map with precision the interconnectedness of living beings. A few Western and Eastern philosophers intuited an interdependent web of sentient beings, but those intuitions could not be documented, so those who subscribed to them were labeled "romantic," "soft," or "nature worshippers" by so-called hard-headed philosophers. But now the tangible effects of environmental crises such as the disappearance of the rain forests, the extinction of animal species, the pollution of air, food, and water can be measured.

Our society creates a particular *need* for belief in the resurrection of body because bodies of all living creatures and the earth's body are disastrously undervalued, abused and manipulated in daily life in our society. Instead of struggling to believe with our rational minds, for intelligent bodies to believe this doctrine is to commit ourselves to living *toward* it—in fact, to seek, *in the present*, to live into the resurrection body. This is both a more realistic and a more demanding definition of belief than that of rational mind's consent.

Augustine had a great respect for acknowledged ignorance. His most often quoted scriptural verse throughout his writings was 1 Corinthians 13:12: "We see now through a glass darkly; then, however, face to face" (*Videmus nunc per speculum in aenigmate; tunc autem facie ad faciem*). As human beings with limited knowledge and perspectives, we are always uncertain, even about the most crucial matters. We do not know the generously responsible way to address the particular situations in which we find ourselves. We always pursue the good *in the dark, by faith*, not knowing for sure what it looks like or feels like; sometimes we do not even recognize it when we see it. Nevertheless, fear that we do not possess certain knowledge must not prevent our passionate commitment to "making love." Belief in the resurrection of body can serve to stimulate our attention and our activity, our *work*, to direct resources to the present suffering of bodies. Theologian Reinhold Niebuhr wrote,

> Nothing worth doing can be achieved in a lifetime; therefore we must be saved by hope. Nothing that is true or beautiful or good makes complete sense in any immediate context of history; therefore we must be saved by faith. Nothing that we do, however virtuous, can be accomplished alone; therefore we are saved by love.[23]

23. Quoted by Sifton, *Serenity Prayer*, 349.

8

Intelligent Bodies Die

Life is not undone by death—nor a single
moment by all the moments that come after it.
—WAYNE JOHNSTON[1]

One must feel the washing of the tide over all that
has been so meticulously sketched by hand.
—JOYCE SCHULD[2]

Is it different to die as an intelligent body rather than
as a compound of immortal soul and disposable body?
From Plato onward, centuries of instruction on "the art
of dying" advocate the study of philosophy—the development and exercise of the rational mind—as effective
"practice for dying." Maxine Sheets-Johnstone identifies
the pursuit of *more*, greed, as the source of the "immor-

---

1. Johnston, *Navigator of New York*, 467.
2.. Schuld, *Augustine and the Hermeneutics of Fragility*, 125.

tality ideologies" promoted and sustained by cultures.[3] David Loy explains that because the ego senses and fears that "I am not real," we seek to establish our reality by acquisition and by denying the physical reality of death. The ego-self, preoccupied with making itself real, is a product of the isolated rational mind.[4]

> The letting go that is necessary is not directly accessible to consciousness. . . . The ego is that which believes itself to be alive and fears death; hence the ego, *although only a mental construction,* will face its immanent disappearance with horror. Uncovering that repression, recovering the denial of death for consciousness, requires the courage to suffer. Our struggle against death is usually redirected into symbolic games of competition, as the urge to defeat our opponent or at least be a little better than our neighbor. To free us from the paralysis of death-in-life, the energy which is distorted into such symptomatic activities must be translated back into its more original form, the terror of death, and that terror endured.[5]

If, however, the person does not identify with the ego precariously constructed by rational mind, the ego-self collapses into the immediacy of *life. Becoming real,* the project of rational mind, dissolves in the urgency of the living intelligent body.

3.. Sheets-Johnstone, *Roots of Morality,* 16.

4. Ibid., 158. Sheets-Johnstone acknowledges that "the mere fact of being alive carries with it a desire for *more.*" I agree that the ego-project of immortality must be jettisoned, without, however, relinquishing the goal of *more life.*

5. Loy, *Lack and Transcendence,* 57.

What does the intelligent body have to say about the immortality project? Endeavoring to think as an intelligent body, I immediately notice that the intelligent body's project is *not the ego's immortality*, but simply *more life*—a different kind of *more*—not the acquisitive grasping of belongings and achievements sought by the ego-self. The newborn infant's first (involuntary) act is to gasp/grasp for breath/life. Throughout life, the intelligent body's most primitive instinct is to struggle for life, whether for breath or for physical healing. Augustine recognized the lifelong longing for more life.

This longing does not emerge from an "immortality ideology" based in an isolated rational mind, but in the organs and cells of the intelligent body. *Immortality ideologies translate intelligent body's inarticulate longing for more life into rational mind's idiom, language.* (Over)valuing soul/rational mind as we do, we define ourselves by its assumptions and proposals. Rational mind bargains to sacrifice body for the immortality of soul/rational mind.

We should not, I believe, self-identify with *either* of our alleged components. Rather we must practice *thinking* with the intelligent body, the body that knows itself and the world but has little practice articulating its knowledge, usually assigning thought to the rational mind. Death occurs when the intelligent body perishes, no longer able to gasp/grasp life. "Well then, has life perished? No, certainly not. . . . It is simply no longer *there*."[6] This—the whirling life of the universe—*is more life*, is the "immortality" of the intelligent body. What tangible difference does the desire for *more life* rather than an im-

6. Plotinus, *Ennead* 4.5.7.

mortality ideology make in the dying experience of an intelligent body? Consider first the centaur's death.

The Centaur's Death

A practical effect of immortality ideologies is the modern medical commitment to conquering death. Descartes' *cogito ergo sum,* which has been called a "founding gesture of the modern age," posits a subject with mastery over all objects.[7] Because of this assumption, Eric Krakauer suggests, "Science presupposes a world of objects that are susceptible to measurement, calculation, exposure, comprehension, and mastery."[8] He argues convincingly that Descartes' identification of the thinking subject authorizes modern medical practice, understood as "securing and maintaining the preeminent good of health by mastering the body and its diseases."[9] This model of medicine assumes that, in principle, death can be deferred indefinitely. In practice, however, this project has "prolonged and complicated dying and propagated suffering."[10] Such technologies as feeding tubes, drugs, mechanical ventilators, hemodialysis machines, and artificial hydration hold inevitable death temporarily at bay at the cost of increasing and extending suffering.

> Deferring death becomes more important than attending to the soul or preparation for the afterlife or the next life; it becomes more important

7. Krakauer, "To Be Freed," 389.

8. Ibid., 385–86.

9. Ibid., 387.

10. Ibid., 388.

than being with or saying farewell to loved ones, reconciling with estranged loved ones, or being home; it becomes more important even than a patient's inability to do any of these tasks.[11]

The centaur's death is a "harsh and acerbic" experience, the "separation of the soul from the body." If we understand ourselves as components, we experience death as Augustine described it:[12]

For a sensation of anguish, contrary to nature, is produced by the force that tears apart the two things that had been conjoined and interwoven during life; and this sensation persists until there is a complete cessation of all that feeling which was present by reason of the union of soul and flesh.[13]

The Dying Intelligent Body

How does the intelligent body's death differ from the painful death of the centaur? It is not the violent rending of the "parts" of the person, but the death of the whole person, the intelligent body. Christians believe that the whole person dies *in the hope* of resurrection of the whole. People who do not share this hope can die trusting that the life they have shared will continue to participate, in some unknown way, in the life of the universe. Mastery of death, transcendence, or victory over death are not the

11. Ibid., 390.
12. Ibid., 388, 390; Augustine, *City of God*, 13.6.
13. *City of God*, 13.6.

intelligent body's goals. William Cullen Bryant imagined the intelligent body's death as follows:

> So live that thou go not, like the quarry-slave at night,
> Scourged to his dungeon, but, sustain'd and soothed
> By an unfaltering trust, approach thy grave
> Like one who wraps the drapery of his couch
> About him, and lies down to pleasant dreams.[14]

In hospice training I learned that most people who are near death have two fears: pain and being alone. Hospice exists to respond to both fears. Hospice volunteers stay with a dying patient, in shifts if necessary; and the patient need not suffer. Of course, pain relief comes at the expense of consciousness, and many patients negotiate for less than complete pain relief in order to maintain a degree of consciousness.

Hospice, an organization committed to palliative medicine, focuses on patients' suffering and its alleviation. Palliative care is the alternative to modern medicine's project of "mastering" death by indefinitely delaying it. It "*lets dying be*."[15] Palliative medicine uses technologies that do not aim at a cure, but at alleviating suffering.[16] Suffering is understood to include not only physical suffering but also the patient's feelings of loss—loss of ability to function, loss of loved ones, loss of the beautiful natural word, and finally, loss of one's individual life itself. Although hospice organizations originated in the nineteenth century, until the middle of that century all

14. Bryant, "Thanatopsis."
15. Krakauer, "To Be Freed," 391.
16. Ibid.

hospitals were, in effect, hospices in which dying patients were treated both physically and spiritually. Hospice programs are presently becoming popular as an alternative to medical care that seeks to prolong life:

> In less than forty years, America has moved from a minimum number of patients treated and dying in hospices to, in 2009, nearly 42% of all deaths (1.2 million) occurring in a hospice program. Between 2000 and 2008, the number of hospital-palliative care programs grew exponentially . . .[17]

Nevertheless,

> in 2010 nearly 60% of patients who died in America—2,450,000—did not have the vital assistance of palliative care professionals to make their final days less stressful and less painful.[18]

My brother Wendell, at the age of fifty-nine, died of endocarditis on April 22, 2010.[19] I had been with him in the hospital for several days, talking with doctors and with his longtime companion, Rita. When he became ill, Wendell told family members emphatically that if he had "something bad" he would not accept surgery and did not want to be in a nursing facility for the rest of his life. Wendell had thought through his wishes; in his journal, he wrote, "When a person chooses to say that he has had enough of life it should at least be accepted, if not

---

17. Ball, *At Liberty to Die*, 3.

18. Ibid., 11.

19. My book *The Wendell Cocktail: Mental Illness, Addiction, and Beauty* describes his life and death.

respected. People should be able to do as they choose as long as others are not intentionally hurt."[20]

As his eldest sibling I had to make the decision to take him off life support, a decision that quite clearly followed his wishes but was excruciating nevertheless. The neurologist showed us X-rays of the several strokes Wendell had had and was continuing to have. Both sides of his brain had blood clots and swelling. The blood would eventually be reabsorbed, the neurologist said, but it made no sense to keep him alive if he had refused to have the necessary valve replacement surgery. The doctor explained the best-case scenario: *if* he had valve replacement surgery, *and if* he worked very hard for at least a year, he *might* regain 30 percent of his mental and physical capacity. But he would be in a nursing home for the rest of his life.

After life supports were removed, he breathed with difficulty for two days. He was unresponsive, with open eyes but seeing nothing. Shortly before he died the neurologist who had explained his condition came to his room. I was sitting alone with Wendell, holding his hand. The doctor laid his hand on my shoulder in sympathy. At the time I appreciated the gesture more than his words, but later I realized that he was telling me, by describing how terribly damaged Wendell's body was, that I had made the right decision in removing him from life support.

At about 12:30 A.M. Wendell's breathing became very light; soon there were six to ten seconds between

---

20. Miles, *Wendell Cocktail*, 49. Elsewhere in his journal, Wendell wrote, "Patients have a right to refuse treatment. Doctors cannot touch you if you tell them, no thank you, I don't want your help. I want no force outside myself to tell me what I have to do. I need to control my body and mind; legally I have this right" (ibid., 74).

breaths. Then they stopped. Although I hadn't called her, a nurse came into the room. I told her that I thought he had stopped breathing and she began to massage his chest strongly and call him, "Wendell, Wendell!" I said, "Oh, please don't pull him back. For what?"

Palliative care does not aim at cure; if a new medicine is discovered that has a chance at reversing a patient's terminal illness, the patient is at liberty to leave hospice in order to try the new drug. If, however, the patient decides that she has had enough of life, she should be able to choose "death with dignity." Howard Ball's *At Liberty to Die* describes the successful legal battles for "death with dignity" in the states of Oregon, Washington, and Montana. He discusses the court rulings and the passionate catch phrases characterizing both sides of the battle for and against the legalization of physician-assisted death (PAD). Those who oppose PAD, he argues, neglect to pay attention to "the person who is dying and in great pain or without *any* quality of life." He urges a "culture of *compassion*" focused on the suffering of the dying instead of the arguments brought by the "culture of life" proponents, who target supporters of PAD as representing the "culture of death."[21] Language is a powerful tool. These slogans obscure the values embedded in them. As proponents of palliative care claim, "death with dignity" proponents argue that those who insist on "medicalization of death" attempt to "master" death by interventions that extend and complicate dying.[22]

---

21. Ball, *At Liberty to Die*, 169.
22. Ibid., 22.

> Compassion reflects the ability to personalize
> and feel for the person who is dying and in great
> pain or without *any* quality of life. . . . And when
> the battles in the states focus on culture of life
> versus culture of death, there is an objectifica-
> tion of the dilemma. . . . We tend to forget the
> plight of the individual who is dying but does
> not yet have the liberty to die under his own
> terms. However, until there is a backing off the
> vitriolic language used by both sides, there is,
> I fear, little hope of bypassing these slogans in
> the political and legal battles for physician as-
> sistance in dying.[23]

The most vocal and wealthy voice of opposition to
PAD is the Roman Catholic Church. Through its spokes-
men the Catholic Church has accused those who advocate the provision of "death with dignity" of disrespecting
and ignoring the "value of human life."[24] They argue that
legalizing PAD will establish a slippery slope, leading
first to voluntary, then involuntary euthanasia of patients.[25] However, this has not proven to be the case in the
states in which PAD has been legalized: Oregon (1994),
Washington (2008), and Montana (2009).

Catholic opposition is puzzling, for several reasons.
First, in the early centuries of the Commom Era, when
Christianity was an illegal cult of the Roman Empire, its
heroes were Christians who chose martyrdom rather than
abjure their faith. Choosing martyrdom for Christian
faith, however, was never understood as "choosing death,"
even though tossing a few grains of incense on a fire below

23. Ibid., 169.
24. Ibid., 153.
25. Ibid., 164.

the emperor's portrait would suffice to avoid death. To the contrary, it was seen by Christians as a choice for *more life*.[26] Yet throughout the history of debate over PAD, death with dignity has been understood as "choosing death," both by its proponents and by Christian opposition.

Second, Christians' belief in the resurrection of body assumes that death is not the end, and is never the goal of human life. The arguments are wrongly cast: Should dying people have the opportunity to "choose death over life"? The Roman Catholic Church, after all, professes to believe that a dying person passes "out of death to life." Presently, after many centuries of explicitly affirmed belief in the resurrection of body, the Catholic Church officially sees only death in PAD. In fact, the dying person is not in a position to "choose" life or death; the only choice is death with dignity, or a helpless and unnecessarily painful death.

There is another alternative to the "choice of death over life." For people who cannot believe in the Christian affirmation of life after death, the third-century Platonic philosopher Plotinus describes a secular faith that does not depend on a supernatural source. Plotinus's argument, put simply, is that at death, life does not perish; rather, *"life goes on."* At death, life abandons the dying body to animate other forms. Like light (Plotinus's example), life depends on its universal source, not on the body animated by it. A person, then, should most fruitfully identify, not with body, but with the source, the immense rushing universe of life. "When the body perishes . . . how could the life still remain? Well, then, has this life

26. Ibid., 163.

perished? No, certainly not, for this too is the image of a radiance; it is simply no longer *there*."[27]

Intelligent bodies have a different experience of death than does the centaur. Not clinging to an immortality ideology, but longing for *more life,* the vast, pulsating life of the universe, the intelligent body can fling itself into that life. Plotinus wrote, "When he has nowhere to set himself and limit himself and determine how far he himself goes, he will stop marking himself off from all being and will come to the All without going out anywhere, but remaining there where the All is set firm. . . . One and the same life holds the sphere."[28]

The universe, Plotinus said, is "boiling over with life."[29] The many forms of life participate in the one life of the universe. "Because you approached the All and did not remain in a part of it, and you did not even say of yourself 'I am just so much,' but by rejecting the 'so much' you have become all."[30]

27. Plotinus, *Ennead* 4.5.7.
28. Ibid., 6.5.7.
29. Ibid., 6.5.12.
30. Ibid., 6.5.9.

Epilogue

> If the truest life is life by thought, and is the
> same thing as the truest thought, then the truest
> thought lives, and contemplation, and the object
> of contemplation at this level, is living and life,
> and the two together are one.
>
> —PLOTINUS[1]

Life offers many opportunities to get over oneself; these opportunities seem to be especially concentrated in hospice volunteering. Hospice volunteers learn to *hold together* several apparent contradictions. In our training, the answer to our anxious questions about hypothetical situations was often, "Just be yourself." But intimacy with strangers in the last supremely personal moments of their lives also requires the opposite: "Get over yourself." Both are true and there is no way to resolve the contradiction in language. It can be resolved only "on location," that is, in being *with* the patient. Augustine wrote a version of this thought in a letter: "We must bend easily lest we break" (*flectamur facile non frangamur*).[2]

1. *Ennead* 3.8.8.
2. Augustine, *Epistula* 104. 3. 11.

115

Auguste Rodin, *Elle qui fut la belle heaulmière*
(*She who was the helmet maker's once-beautiful wife*),
a figure in *The Gates of Hell* (1886)³

3. 50 x 30 x 26.5

The fourteenth-century German mystic Meister Eckhart wrote, "The more ourselves we are, the less self there is in us." I came to understand something of what he meant in my experience of hospice volunteering. I became "more myself" as I recognized that my patient and I both participate conditionally in life. It is as accurate to say that I am a dying person as it is to say that she is a living person. She has lived in the part of the life cycle that I presently inhabit, and someday I will live in the part of the lifecycle in which she now lives. I have "less self" when the boundaries between myself and another person soften and become permeable. Simultaneously I am "more self" when I live not just in the present moment, but in my whole life.

The model for Rodin's bronze sculpture *She who was the helmet maker's once-beautiful wife* came from Italy to Paris on foot to see her son, one of Rodin's models. Rodin asked her to pose for this remarkable sculpture. The aged female body has seldom been seen as a worthy subject for art, and we do not know Rodin's motivation in using her as a model. He sculpted many conventionally beautiful female (and male) bodies; perhaps he saw this body as beautiful also. The intricate planes and shadows of her body must have fascinated him. Critics see sadness and ugliness in her shrunken breasts and bloated belly.[4] I see beauty in a body that tells the truth about time.

Philosopher Susanne Langer observed that a person's affective life is trained by the "arts" we live with daily. For most Americans that is the media, which trains our

4. See the Web site of the Musée Rodin: http://www.musee-rodin.fr/en/collections/sculptures/she-who-was-helmet-makers-once-beautiful-wife.

eyes to identify as beautiful bodies that are young, untouched by living. Yet in the long adventure of life, both joy and suffering mark the body. As a seventysomething woman, I am not yet the intelligent body of *la belle heaulmière*. But if I am fortunate I will get there. Several years ago I undertook an exercise; I attempted to overcome my own socialization to what female beauty looks like by looking long and intently each day at a photograph of this sculpture. I had a very personal reason for undertaking this exercise; I wanted not to feel ugly as an old woman. I wanted to "get over myself," that is, my socialization to see the body of *la belle heaulmière* as ugly. It was easy to see the *sculpture* as beautiful, but I wanted to see not only the sculpture but the *body itself* as beautiful. It took about a year, but I now see—at the level of *perception* not judgment[5]—this fully inhabited body, the site of a lifetime of experience, as utterly beautiful.

Compare this sculpture with Rodin's more famous *The Thinker*, whose heavily muscled body communicates strength. Both figures are absorbed in thought, curved into themselves, engrossed in subjectivity. Neither is posed; there is no eye contact with viewers. Neither sculpture's facial expression defines his/her thought/feeling; both bodies express concentrated interiority. Neither figure is a centaur! Both are intelligent bodies. *The Thinker* struggles to pull a thought from his straining body. *La belle heaulmière* reflects quietly on her long experience. Intelligent bodies are beautiful.

5. Leonardo da Vinci is reported to have said, "The organ of perception acts more quickly than the judgment."

It will take more than a book to dislodge a figure as deeply embedded in the psyche of the West as that of the centaur. Because the stacked components model of person appears to match common experience, we do not pause to examine critically its effects, even while these pervade our lives, shaping our experience. Assuming the accuracy of the inherited model, we neglect to seek a model that would serve us better. In fact, we do not recognize the extent to which we already *do* treat others as intelligent bodies, imagining (accurately or inaccurately) the life experiences their bodies reveal as we listen to their words. Nevertheless, when someone asks us to define "person," we are likely to cite some version of the ancient components model. There is a disconnect between our experience as intelligent bodies and rational mind's interpretation of who we are as persons.

This book has proposed another model—Maxine Sheets-Johnstone's groundbreaking description of the intelligent body. I hope that I have demonstrated the greater accuracy and myriad advantages—both intimate and social—of this model. We think of others as intelligent bodies only to the extent that we understand ourselves in this way. We can *perceive* ourselves and others as rational minds stubbornly defending certain *ideas* and trying to overlook insubordinate bodies. Or we can think of ourselves and others as whole persons, directed—led—to the beauty and significance of our lives by the particular *experiences* by which we are shaped, by the people we have loved and who have loved us, by the circumstances of our childhood, and by the arts we choose to live with daily. It will not be easy to think of ourselves and others as intelligent bodies against the vast unquestioned consensus that we are uneasily composed of unequally valued *components*. But as Plato recognized, "All that is beautiful is difficult."[6]

6. Plato, *Greater Hippias* 204e.

Bibliography

Althaus-Reid, Marcella Maria, and Lisa Isherwood, eds. *Controversies in Body Theology*. London: SCM, 2008.

Arendt, Hannah. *Thinking*. The Life of the Mind 1. New York: Harcourt Brace Jovanovich, 1971.

———. *Willing*. The Life of the Mind 2. New York: Harcourt Brace Jovanovich, 1978.

Augustine, Saint. *An Augustine Synthesis*. Arranged by Erich Przywara. New York: Harper, 1958.

———. *The City of God against the Pagans*. Edited and translated by R. W. Dyson. Cambridge: Cambridge University Press, 1998.

———. *Confessions*. Translated by Rex Warner. New York: New American Library, 1963.

———. *Later Works*. Selected and translated by John Burnaby. Library of Christian Classics 8. Philadelphia: Westminster, 1955.

Ball, Howard. *At Liberty to Die: The Battle for Death with Dignity in America*. New York: New York University Press, 2012.

Becker, Dana. *The Myth of Empowerment: Women and the Therapeutic Culture in America*. New York: New York University Press, 2005.

Becker, Ernest. *The Denial of Death*. New York: Free Press, 1975.

Bonaventure, Saint. *The Mind's Road to God*. Translated by George Boas. New York: Liberal Arts, 1953.

Brown, David. *Tradition and Imagination: Revelation and Change*. Oxford: Oxford University Press,1999.

Brown, Norman O. *Life against Death: The Psychoanalytical Meaning of History*. 1st ed. Middleton, CT: Weslyan University Press, 1959.

Bussanich, John. "Plotinus's Metaphysics of the One." In *The Cambridge Companion to Plotinus*, edited by Lloyd P. Gerson, 38–65. New York: Cambridge University Press, 1996.

Chadwick, Owen, ed. *Western Asceticism*. Library of Christian Classics 12. Philadelphia: Westminster, 1958.

Bibliography

Copeland, M. Shawn. *Enfleshing Freedom: Body, Race, and Being.* Minneapolis: Fortress, 2010.

Corin, Ellen. "The 'Other' of Culture in Psychosis: The Ex-Centricity of the Subject." In *Subjectivity: Ethnographic Investigations,* edited by João Biehl, Byron Good, and Arthur Kleinman, 273–314. Berkeley: University of California Press, 2007.

Damasio, Antonio. *Descartes' Error: Emotion, Reason and the Human Brain.* New York: HarperCollins, 1994.

——. *The Feeling of What Happens: Body and Emotion in the Making of Consciousness.* 1st ed. New York: Harcourt Brace, 1999.

Descartes, René. *Discourse on the Method of Rightly Conducting the Reason, and Seeking Truth in the Sciences.* Great Books of the Western World 31. Chicago: Encyclopedia Britannica, 1952.

——. *Meditations on First Philosophy.* Great Books of the Western World 31. Chicago: Encyclopedia Britannica, 1952.

Dreyfus, Hubert L., and Paul Rabinow, eds. *Michel Foucault: Beyond Structuralism and Hermeneutics.* Chicago: University of Chicago Press, 1982.

Elie, Paul. "Has Fiction Lost Its Faith?" *New York Times Book Review,* December 23, 2012, http://www.nytimes.com/2012/12/23/books/review/has-fiction-lost-its-faith.html?_r=0.

Foucault, Michel. *Discipline and Punish: The Birth of the Prison.* Translated by Alan Sheridan. New York: Vintage, 1979.

——. *The Foucault Reader.* Edited by Paul Rabinow. New York: Pantheon, 1984.

Glancy, Jennifer A. *Slavery in Early Christianity.* New York: Oxford University Press, 2002.

Glucklich, Ariel. *Sacred Pain: Hurting the Body for the Sake of the Soul.* New York: Oxford University Press, 2001.

Green, Joel B. *Body, Soul, and Human Life: The Nature of Humanity in the Bible.* Grand Rapids: Baker Academic, 2008.

Hartouni, Valerie. *Visualizing Atrocity: Arendt, Evil, and the Optics of Thoughtlessness.* New York: New York University Press, 2012.

Haug, Frigga. *Female Sexualization: A Collective Work of Memory.* London: Verso, 1987.

Hennessy, Rosemary. *Profit and Pleasure: Sexual Identities in Late Capitalism.* New York: Routledge, 2000.

Holt, James. "Two Brains Running." *New York Times Book Review,* November 27, 2011, 16–17.

Hunt, Lynn. *Inventing Human Rights: A History.* New York: Norton, 2007.

Bibliography

Hustveldt, Siri. *The Sorrows of an American*. New York: Henry Holt, 2008.

John Damascene, Saint. *Barlaam and Joasaph*. Translated by G. R. Woodward and H. Mattingly. London: W. Heinemann, 1914.

Johnson, Wayne. *The Navigator of New York*. New York: Doubleday, 2002.

Kirsch, Adam. "On Bellow's *Henderson the Rain King*." *New York Review of Books*, December 6, 2012, http://www.nybooks.com/articles/archives/2012/dec/06/bellows-henderson-rain-king/?pagination=false.

Krakauer, Eric. "To Be Freed from the Infirmity of (the) Age: Subjectivity, Life-Sustaining Treatment, and Palliative Medicine." In *Subjectivity: Ethnographic Investigations*, edited by João Biehl, Byron Good, and Arthur Kleinman, 381–96. Berkeley: University of California Press, 2007.

Kristeva, Julia. *Powers of Horror: An Essay on Abjection*. New York: Columbia University Press, 1982.

LaMothe, Kimerer. *Family Planting: A Farm-Fed Philosophy of Human Relations*. Lanham, MD: O Books, 2011.

Langer, Susanne. *Philosophical Sketches*. New York: Mentor, 1962.

Leder, Drew. *The Absent Body*. Chicago: University of Chicago Press, 1990.

Leeuw, Gerardus van der. *Sacred and Profane Beauty: The Holy in Art*. Translated by David E. Green. New York: Oxford University Press, 2006.

Liew, Tat-siong Benny, ed. *Reading Ideologies: Essays on the Bible and Interpretation in Honor of Mary Ann Tolbert*. Sheffield: Sheffield Phoenix, 2011.

Loy, David. *Lack and Transcendence: The Problem of Life and Death in Psychotherapy, Existentialism, and Buddhism*. New York: Humanity Books, 2000.

MacFarquhar, Larissa. "Two Heads: A Marriage Devoted to the Mind-Body Problem." *New Yorker*, February 12, 2007, 58–69.

Manschreck, Clyde L. *Melanchthon: The Quiet Reformer*. New York: Abingdon, 1958.

Marion, Jean-Luc. *God Without Being*. Translated by Thomas A. Carlson. Chicago: University of Chicago Press, 1999.

Miles, Margaret R. *Augustine and the Fundamentalist's Daughter*. Eugene, OR: Cascade, 2011.

———. *Augustine on the Body*. Missoula, MT: Scholars, 1979.

———. *Carnal Knowing: Female Nakedness and Religious Meaning in the Christian West*. Boston: Beacon, 1989.

———. *Plotinus on Body and Beauty: Society, Philosophy, and Religion in Third-Century Rome*. Oxford: Blackwell, 1999.

———. *The Wendell Cocktail: Mental Illness, Addiction, and Beauty*. Eugene, OR: Cascade, 2011.

———. *The Word Made Flesh: A History of Christian Thought*. Oxford: Blackwell, 2005.

Miller, Patricia Cox. *The Corporeal Imagination: Signifying the Holy in Late Ancient Christianity*. Philadelphia: University of Pennsylvania Press, 2009.

Miringoff, Marc, and Marque-Luisa Miringoff, with Sandra Opdycke. *The Social Health of the Nation: How America Is Really Doing*. New York: Oxford University Press, 1999.

Mohrmann, Christine. *Etudes sur le latin des chrétiens*. Vol. 3. Roma: Edizioni di Storia E Letteratura, 1965.

Musurillo, Herbert, ed. *Acts of the Christian Martyrs*. New York: Oxford University Press, 1972.

Nussbaum, Martha. *Hiding from Humanity: Disgust, Shame, and the Law*. Princeton: Princeton University Press, 2004.

Pangle, Thomas L., ed. *The Roots of Political Philosophy: Ten Forgotten Socratic Dialogues*. Ithaca: Cornell University Press, 1987.

Pascal, Blaise. *Pensées*. Translated by A. J. Krailsheimer. Harmondsworth, UK: Penguin, 1966.

Perkins, Judith. *The Suffering Self: Pain and Narrative Representation in the Early Christian Era*. London: Routledge, 1995.

Pfister, Joel. *Staging Depth: Eugene O'Neill and the Politics of Psychological Discourse*. Chapel Hill: University of North Carolina Press, 1995.

Plato. *Collected Dialogues*. Edited by Edith Hamilton and Huntington Cairns. Princeton: Princeton University Press, 1961.

Plotinus. *Enneads*. Translated by A. H. Armstrong. 7 vols. Loeb Classical Library. Cambridge: Harvard University Press, 1966–88.

Porter, James I., ed. *Constructions of the Classical Body*. Ann Arbor: University of Michigan Press, 2002.

Richlin, Amy. "Cicero's Head." In *Constructions of the Classical Body*, edited by James I. Porter, 190–211. Ann Arbor: University of Michigan Press, 2002.

Rorty, Richard. "Is Derrida a Transcendental Philosopher?" *Yale Journal of Criticism* 2 (1989) 207–17.

Scarry, Elaine. *The Body in Pain: The Making and Unmaking of the World*. Oxford: Oxford University Press, 1985.

Schuld, Joyce. *Augustine and the Hermeneutics of Fragility.* Notre Dame: University of Notre Dame Press, 2003.

Sheets-Johnstone, Maxine. *The Corporeal Turn: An Interdisciplinary Reader.* Exeter: Imprint Academic, 2009.

———. *The Roots of Morality.* University Park: Pennsylvania State University Press, 2008.

Sifton, Elisabeth. *The Serenity Prayer: Faith and Politics in Times of Peace and War.* New York: Norton, 2003.

Smail, Daniel Lord. *On Deep History and the Brain.* Berkeley: University of California Press, 2008.

Stein, Arlene. *Shameless: Sexual Dissidence in American Culture.* New York: New York University Press, 2006.

Stevens, Wallace. *Collected Poems.* 1st collected ed. New York: Knopf, 1978.

Thomas, à Kempis. *The Imitation of Christ.* Translated by Betty I. Knott. London: Collins, 1963.

Traherne, Thomas. *Centuries of Meditations.* Edited by Bertram Dobell. London: Dobell, 1948.

Trott, Susan. *The Holy Man's Journey.* New York: Riverhead, 1997.

Vance, Richard P. "Medical Ethics in the Absence of a Moral Consensus." *B & R Reviews*, December 1986, 5, 12.

Vetlesen, Arne Johan. *Perception, Empathy, and Judgment: An Inquiry into the Preconditions of Moral Performance.* University Park: Pennsylvania State University Press, 1994.

Vollmar, Valerie, ed. "Recent Developments in Physician-Assisted Death." http://www.willamette.edu/wucl/pdf/pas/2009.pdf.

Wesley, John. *The Journal of John Wesley: A Selection.* Edited by Elisabeth Jay. New York: Oxford University Press, 1987.

Wheelwright, Philip E., ed. *The Presocratics.* New York: Odyssey, 1966.

Subject Index

Name Index

Made in the USA
Middletown, DE
02 January 2018